CADOGAN
gourmet guides

lazy days out
in Andalucía

Cadogan Books plc
London House, Parkgate Road,
London SW11 4NQ, UK

Distributed in the USA by
The Globe Pequot Press
6 Business Park Road, PO Box 833, Old Saybrook,
Connecticut 06475-0833

Copyright © Jeremy Wayne, Dana Facaros and Michael Pauls 1996
Illustrations © Charles Shearer 1996
Book, cover and map design by Animage
Cover photography and illustration by Horacio Monteverde
Maps © Cadogan Guides, drawn by Animage and Map Creation Ltd

Series editor: Rachel Fielding
Editing: Antony Mason

Additional editing and proof-reading: Fiona Clarkson Webb
    cookery: Michelle Clark

DTP: Linda McQueen and Kicca Tommasi
Production: Rupert Wheeler Book Production Services
Printed and bound in the UK by Redwood Books Ltd , Trowbridge

ISBN 1-86011-060-6
A catalogue record for this book is available from the British Library

All rights reserved. No part of this publication may be reproduced, stored in a retrieval system, or transmitted, in any form or by any means, electronic or mechanical, including photocopying and recording, or by any information storage and retrieval system except as may be expressly permitted by the UK 1988 Copyright Design & Patents Act and the USA 1976 Copyright Act or in writing from the publisher. Requests for permission should be addressed to Cadogan Books plc, London House, Parkgate Road, London SW11 4NQ.

Please help us keep this guide up to date

Every effort has been made to ensure the accuracy of the information in this book at the time of going to press. However, standards in restaurants and practical details such as opening times and, in particular, prices are liable to change. We would be delighted to receive any comments concerning existing entries or indeed any suggestions for inclusion in future editions or companion volumes. Significant contributions will be acknowledged in the next edition, and authors of the best letters will receive a copy of the Cadogan Guide of their choice.

The author and publishers have made every effort to ensure the accuracy of the information in the book at the time of going to press. However, they cannot accept any responsibility for any loss, injury or inconvenience resulting from the use of information contained in this guide.

About the Author

Jeremy Wayne is a freelance food and travel writer. He is a regular contributor to the *Sunday Times* and *The Oldie*, and writes *The Guide*'s weekly *Eating Out* page for the Saturday *Guardian*. He first visited Andalucía in 1967 and now divides his time between Spain and England.

Acknowledgements

Many people have helped to make this book possible, but special thanks are due to Diana Serop of the Patronato de Turismo, Costa del Sol; Pepe Cervi and his staff at British Airways, Málaga; the concierges of Hotel Los Monteros; Marilyn Gordon; Santos and Marianne Dominguez, and Shaida and Francisco at The Travel Shop; in London, Rachel Fielding at Cadogan for her endless patience, and Antony Mason, who has edited this guide so expertly, for his; and most of all to my wife Tara who not only listened to and corrected my clumsy text but climbed mountains, crossed rivers, braved storms, and accompanied me always, without complaint, in the wettest winter since records began, to Andalucía's far-flung corners in the unceasing search for good food.

Dana Facaros and Michael Pauls, who have contributed significantly to the Touring Around sections of this book, used to live in Granada and have written over 20 guide books for Cadogan. They now live in a leaky old farmhouse in southwest France with their two children and assorted animals.

Contents

Introduction

Marguerite Alphandery N. Y. 8-23-96

I first came to Andalucía as a child, on a family holiday in 1967. A year later we were back, more adventurous this time, motoring from the Algarve in Portugal, across the Guadiana river to Huelva and the wetlands of Las Marismas. In Sevilla the splendours of the cathedral and Alcázar failed to excite me. But I was held in thrall by the *tapas* bars of this great city, platters piled high with brindled gastropods, cream-coloured quail's eggs smooth as ivory, fat yellow mussels in violet shells, and silvery fishes winking, so it seemed, especially at me. At the age of ten, this precocious child lived through his stomach. Even tourist restaurants, the kind with menus in four languages, each indexed with a well-thumbed flag, were to me very temples of delight. These days such multilingual dishes may sound less than tempting, but then I found them irresistible—*soup with fried egges, fisch in the way of the house, custard of the aunt.* I couldn't wait to tuck into them all.

In those unenlightened days, long before the British fell in love with olive oil, and rocket was something you went to the moon in, Spanish food was dismissed as 'oily': and so it was. It still is, of course, only these days we seek it out. The olive was already flourishing in the province of Jaén when Tuscany was

1

still a forest. Hardly surprising that it plays so important a role in the cooking of the South.

In an area which has known crushing poverty for centuries—and the worst of it probably in our own—good restaurants have been slow to evolve. Whereas in most of the English-speaking world we are now learning to cook all over again under the tutelage of celebrity chefs and food writers, in Spain it's the other way around. A tremendously rich and diverse cuisine, good Spanish cooking has always prospered in the home; until recently, it was *confined* to it.

Of course, cities like Madrid have always had their *Horcher* and their *Jockey*, but the grand cuisine of these restaurants was largely imported. Only now is Spain in general, and Andalucía in particular, beginning to realize the value of its own native cooking: the long-awaited Renaissance is finally under way.

Each of Andalucía's eight provinces—Almería, Málaga, Cádiz, Huelva, Sevilla, Córdoba, Jaén and Granada—is blessed with a different storehouse of agricultural products and historical traditions which its cuisine necessarily reflects. The twenty selected restaurants in *Lazy Days Out in Andalucía* are a personal choice, one which aims to cross the board in terms of style and variety. Some, such as *El Churrasco* and *Ruta del Veleta*, offer urban chic; others, such as *Los Cano*, are great examples of their ilk, namely the beachside *chiringuito*; while a few—the remote, welcoming *Huerta de San Rafael* or the Araby *Molienda* at Benalauría, for instance—are genuine discoveries crying out to be shared. Nearly all, by the way, have some kind of view. The prices given are, of course, only approximate, but they are based upon a three-course lunch for one with an *aperitivo* before, or a *digestivo* after; a half-bottle of house wine, a bottle of mineral water, and coffee.

There are some excellent restaurants too that could not be included, usually for reasons of location; either they were too close to others to be practical for the format of this book, or in an unfortunate position which would have meant a meagre accompanying 'touring around' section. A selection of these 'also rans' appears below.

These, and all the restaurants in this guide book, have one thing in common: they love good food as much as you do. From the first *strigueros*, the sprue asparagus of spring, and *alcachofas*—baby artichokes which flourish in the sand dunes—of early summer, to September's larder hung with game birds, venison and wild boar; from winter stews to summer's chilled soups, through succulent meats seared on a charcoal grill to platters of *mariscos*—*langostinas*, *cigalas*, *navajas*, and 100 other molluscs and crustaceans you can never hope to name—the food of Andalucía will delight you all year round. This huge range of raw materials is further enlivened with the gifts of the Moors—cumin, saffron, paprika, turmeric, cinnamon and clove— guaranteed to intoxicate the nostrils and excite the tongue.

Islamic carved panel from the Alhambra

The story, however, is far from universal and, it must be said, many restaurants in Andalucía still have a long way to go. The ubiquitous *caldereta de cordero*, lamb stew, and *albondigas*, meat-balls—the staple hot-dish of *tapas* bars—must be handled with extreme caution. Although there's no excuse for poor meat—the rich grazing pastures of northern Spain produce some of the best in Europe—a good rule of thumb when ordering meat in an unknown restaurant is to inspect it first or ask for it in a form which is readily identifiable.

That said, *tapas* bars are generally excellent, the jewel in Spain's eating-out crown. *Tapas* bars in Andalucía offer a taste of the region, a wide range of flavours, a sampling of different wines or sherries, and the genuine opportunity to talk to local people—all for a few hundred pesetas.

The Spaniards, and especially the Spaniards of the South, as you will read in these chapters, have an impossibly sweet tooth. Perhaps it's a legacy of the Moors. Whatever the cause, the effect is profound. They breakfast on *churros* (spirals of sugared doughnut for dunking into coffee) and neither lunch nor dinner is complete without a sweet dessert. Custards, caramels, meringues and sweet fritters are fine prepared at home, but factory-made and sitting in the chilled display-cabinet of a restaurant, they rather lose their appeal. Spaniards love these chilled cabinets, and while it's always worth asking if desserts are *casera* ('homemade', though this in itself, of course, is no guarantee of quality), remember that in no way does a neon-lit refrigerated cabinet indicate that a restaurant is under-par. It's just a different approach. In so many restaurants the quality of the food may be excellent, but the aesthetics of its presentation are still in their infancy.

Spanish wine is a vast and wonderful subject which can only be touched upon here. Spain is Europe's second largest country and, after Switzerland, its most mountainous. With its variety of climatic contrasts, from snow-covered peaks to scorching valleys, there's one thing common to every region: they all produce wine.

Like everything else in life, you get what you pay for. While there is undoubtedly a certain satisfaction to be derived from finding wine that costs less per bottle than water (and a bottle of *vino de mesa* need cost no more than 150 pts), drinkable wine starts in restaurants at about 700 pts a bottle. If you spend between 1000 pts and 1500 pts, the chances are that you'll be buying quality that would cost twice as much outside Spain. Following on from this, as a general rule, the more expensive the wine, the better the 'bargain'. Instead of saving money, why not splash out on it? The 'splash' will be modest, but you'll get to try some spectacular wines from famous wine-growing areas like Rioja, Navarra and Valdepeñas, as well as local Andalucian ones which hold their own in quality and style. Don't forget sherry, either. The British first developed a taste for it around 500 years ago: drunk with *tapas* and fish, you may soon eschew wine altogether in its favour.

Accompanying the restaurant appraisals in each chapter are 'touring around' sections, with suggestions of ways to complete your lazy (or not quite so lazy) day out. Do as little or as much as you wish; the ethos of this book was that, in terms of sightseeing, *less* would almost certainly be *more*. Take it at your own pace and, if you're remotely serious about any of it, do it in the morning. No self-respecting Andalucian lunches before 2pm—a 4pm start is not unusual—and by the time you've finished, you may find the most appealing sight of all is your hotel bed.

The rebirth of Andalucian cooking is under way, and that small boy in Sevilla, no longer in short trousers but still with appetite unchecked, has returned to investigate further. Those plastic tourist menus are still too much in evidence, but by and large, you eat out extremely well in Andalucía these days. It still needs your encouragement. Seek out good food, praise it and don't get disheartened when you can't find it—it's probably lurking round the corner, in a most unlikely spot hidden from the eye by a tatty Alpujarran curtain. Talk about food—nothing will please a proud chef or restaurant owner more—experiment with it, criticize it and, most of all, enjoy it. As they say round these parts: *¡Buen proveche!*

Also-rans

Here are six recommended restaurants that could not, for reasons explained above, be included as the focus of a Lazy Day Out.

El Almajero, *Explanada del Puerto, Garrucha (Almería), ✆ (95) 046 0405. 3000 pts.*
Super-fresh seafood, the very best in Almería, and a wonderful view of the fishing harbour where the catch is landed.

La Posada, *Gualchos (Granada), ✆ (95) 865 6034. Closed Mon and Dec–Mar. 5500 pts.*
Charming old coaching inn in a delightful white village near the coast east of Motril. José Gonzalez's excellent cooking was the real draw here; now La Posada is about to change hands, let's hope standards remain as high.

Mar de Alborán, *Avenida de Alay 5, Benalmádena-Costa (Málaga), ✆ (95) 244 6427. Closed Sun night, Mon, 24 Dec–22 Jan. 5000 pts.*
The Costa del Sol's finest restaurant—in the Costa del Sol's most disagreeable location. The young chef is a local luminary who cooks sensational Andalucían and Basque dishes with imagination and flair.

Marbella Club Hotel, *Carretera de Cádiz, Marbella (Málaga), ✆ (95) 282 2211. 6000 pts.*
To dine on the terrace of the Marbella Club, in the shade of the cypresses, the air heavy with the scent of jasmine and *dama de noche*, is one of Spain's great sybaritic experiences.

Egaña-Oriza, *San Fernando 41, Sevilla, ✆ (95) 422 7211. Closed Sat lunch, Sun and Aug. 6000 pts.*
Sevilla's most stylish restaurant, set in a magnificent indoor winter garden. Its adjoining, state-of-the-art *tapas* bar offers up-market *tapas* with a Basque flavour to them, and wonderful views across the Jardines del Alcázar.

Da Paolo, *Marina Bay, Gibraltar, ✆ (9567) 76799. £20.*
If you must eat in Gibraltar, eat here. Magnificent view over Gibraltar marina, and if you're lucky the thrill of a British Airways jet taking off or landing just a few hundred yards away. The food, broadly Italian, is the best in Gibraltar.

The Kindliness of Air Conditioning; the Rough Kiss of Firewater

Málaga is the capital of the Costa del Sol, and the main point of entry (at its Pablo Ruiz Picasso airport) for the 2,500,000 visitors who annually flock to Spain's southern shores. Settled first by Phoenicians, later by Romans, and later still by the Moors, this handsome city has seen it all. Its main artery, the Alameda Principal, can hold its own with Nice's Promenade des Anglais for architecture, and the Plaza de la Constitución can match its shops; her slums vie with Naples for poverty, and, after dark, her port area will outdo even Barcelona for sleaze. Look across the perfect curve of the Bay of Málaga to the peaks of the Montes de Málaga beyond, and only the heart of stone could fail to be moved.

It may seem incredible, but 99 per cent of tourists to the Costa del Sol never get to see Málaga. Little do they know what they're missing, for Málaga has so much to offer:

the Alcazaba, Málaga

cathedral, castle, churches, markets, bars and restaurants, *barrios* (districts) of every description—and a beach which seems to go on for ever. And on this beach, in midsummer, you may get to see Málaga's famous Procesión de la Virgen del Carmen, a procession of small boats bearing a life-size Virgin across the water. As day turns into night, the sky explodes into a riot of flares and fireworks. This is Málaga at play. *Malagueños* will tell you it's the most beautiful sight in the world—and at such a moment, the night air heavy with the scent of jasmine and the smell of cordite—there's a fair chance that you'll agree.

You may not be in Málaga in midsummer to experience this, so why not do something else that *malagueños* themselves appreciate: visit one of the restaurants cherished for their efforts to revive the city's fine culinary tradition. For those in the know, there's one place on their lips: Mesón Astorga.

getting there

The restaurant is located on Calle Gerona, in an unprepossessing conglomeration of streets near the centre of Málaga. Three blocks away from Conde de Guadalhorce, it is northwest of the RENFE railway station and south of the Avenida de Andalucía.

Mesón Astorga

Gerona 11, Málaga, ✆ (95) 234 6832. Open daily except Wed 1–4pm and 8–12; booking advisable. About 4500 pts.

Walk into Mesón Astorga at lunch time on a summer's day, when the outside temperature has long since passed the 100°F (38° C) mark, and the air conditioning hits you like a physical barrier. At the long bar, businessmen in sharply pressed lightweight suits down icy *fino* sherry and mentally rehearse strategy while they wait for their appointment to arrive. Two *malagueña mujeres*-who-lunch, their nails as long and as red as chilli peppers, exchange vital information over huge *tintos de verano* before the arrival of the third. She is foolish to be late.

Astorga's interior is a pleasing combination of brick, wood and glass. Opaque, etched windows protect diners from the public view, and add

a 1930s liner feel. Lattice shutters of Moorish design diffuse the glare of the midday sun. All tables in this well-proportioned, square room command a good view, a clever conjuring trick few restaurants seem to get right. Once seated, another drink is *de rigueur* before the waiter will even think to tax you with anything as laborious as a menu.

There's a good selection of both hot and cold starters. The *foie de pato en lecho de escarola*, a smooth, subtle duck pâté served on a bed of endive lettuce is a house speciality. Another is *pastel de rape bañado con huevas de mujol*, a beautifully sophisticated filo tart of monkfish with grey-mullet roes. Astorga specializes too in locally caught tuna—they say 'local' but it's a big, deep-water fish and they have to trawl halfway to North Africa to net it. *Atún plancha con refritos de ajos al vinagre de Jerez*, grilled tuna with fragrant bulbs of garlic and sherry vinegar, is a classic dish here, brimming with three distinct flavours of Andalucía. For meat-eaters, the *magret de pato con salsa de higos al vinagre de frambues*—magret of duck with figs in raspberry vinegar—is another dish upon which Astorga has set its admirable seal.

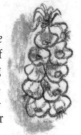

The wine list is somewhat concise for a restaurant of this calibre, but you will find some gems. And while the Riojas, both red and white, are as usual well represented, so too are the wines of Valladolid. A 1991 *Yllera*, at around 1300 pts, has to represent outstanding value for money. With tuna dishes, why not drink salt-tangy Manzanilla sherry throughout?

Business restaurant this may be, but here in Málaga the business of eating and drinking comes first. Indeed, a business lunch is not worthy of the name unless it lasts a good three hours. The pace is slow—and while the young and genial waiters are attentive, they have no wish to rush you. Chances are, by the time dessert comes along you'll be long past it; no bad thing, since sadly the *carta de postres*, with its kitsch colour photographs, does little to inspire. That said, the *crema catalana* is rich, thick, and for once in this country of the impossibly sweet tooth, not too sweet. Time for one of Astorga's myriad *digestivos*. If anis is to your liking, try a local *Pacharán*; they make it up in Periana, 30km away. Or else choose an *aguardiente* from a cast of thousands: it will burn your lips and put fire in your gut.

Crema Catalana

(Serves 4)

750ml/1 ¼ pints milk
100g/4oz cornflour
1 cinnamon stick
zest of 1 lemon
6 egg yolks
175g/6oz caster sugar
2 teaspoons ground cinnamon

Pour a little of the milk into a large mixing bowl and blend the cornflour into it. In a heavy-based saucepan, boil the rest of the milk together with the cinnamon stick and the lemon zest. Meanwhile, thoroughly beat the egg yolks and sugar together.

Remove the cinnamon stick and lemon zest from the pan and stir the boiling milk into the blended cornflour. Rinse the saucepan, return the mixture to it and boil gently for a further 2 minutes. Now remove the pan from the heat, pour in the beaten egg yolk mixture, whisking all the time, then return the pan to a very low heat, still whisking continually, until the custard starts to thicken. This should happen almost immediately.

Pour the custard into a serving bowl, allow to cool, and dust with cinnamon powder before serving.

touring around

Much-maligned **Málaga**, capital not only of the Costa del Sol, but also of crime and sleaze in southern Spain, is making a determined effort to improve its reputation and attract more tourists. In the past, a visit to the swish department store El Corte Inglés may have been the only reason a tourist considered spending any time here at all.

To miss Málaga, however, means to miss the most Spanish of cities, certainly on the Costa del Sol. Whatever you may think of the place, it is alive and real. Ungainly cranes and elegant palm trees compete for dominance of the skyline. Police helicopters roar over the Plaza de la Constitución as pretty Spanish girls toss their skirts and stamp their heels to flamenco music, to a private audience in a public square. Elegant old Spanish ladies, scented with *Maja* soap, sit and reminisce, and dark-eyed tattooed gypsy boys flash their double-edged smiles to lure you into a shoeshine. From its tattered billboards and walls splashed with political slogans, to its public gardens overflowing with exotic fauna, Málaga is a jamboree bag of colours, aromas and sounds. Admittedly it cannot compete with Sevilla or Granada for sheer wealth of cultural distractions, but the *malagueños* are proud of their fun-loving metropolis.

El Corte Inglés, a vast and well-stocked department store, is an easy 15-minute stroll from Mesón Astorga—although in high summer, when temperatures in town really go through the roof, a stroll is never as easy as it might sound. El Corte Inglés is on the Avenida de Andalucía, the main road into Málaga from the west. Where it crosses the dry rocky bed of the Guadalmedina river, just past the department store, it becomes the **Alameda Principal**, a majestic 19th-century boulevard. North of the Alameda is the **Plaza de la Constitución**, in the heart of the commercial centre, and the **Pasaje Chinitas**, an all-and-sundry shopping arcade. One of the clothes shops bears a commemorative plaque signalling that it's the original site of the Café Chinitas, where bullfighters and flamenco singers would gather in the old days; the spirit of it was captured by García Lorca.

The Alameda continues into the **Paseo del Parque**, a tree-lined prom-enade built on reclaimed land that runs along the port area. The park is more than a promenade—it's an area of 30,000 square metres filled with rare and exotic plants, which make up a magnificent botanical garden. You'll see ficus, banana trees, dragon trees and date palms, and, tucked away among them, some magnificent fountains, such as the Renaissance **Fuente Génova** and a 19th-century *malagueño* **Three Graces**. The Paseo leads to the city's **bullring**, built in 1874 with a capacity for 14,000, and very much in use today. Nearby is the **English cemetery**. William Mark, the 19th-century consul, so loved Málaga that he described it as a 'second paradise', and encouraged his fellow countrymen to join him here. In 1830 he founded this ceme-tery, allowing a decent burial to Protestants who had previously been buried on the beach. Hans Christian Andersen declared he could 'well understand how a splenetic Englishman might take his own life in order to be buried in this place.' Its sea views, however, have long since been blocked by concrete buildings.

Just off the Paseo del Parque, the steps lead up to the Moorish fortress, the **Alcazaba**, ✆ (95) 216 0055. Under the Moors, Málaga was the most important port of al-Andalus, and from contemporary references it seems also to have been one of its most beautiful cities. King Fernando thoroughly ruined it in the conquest of 1487, and, after the expulsion of the Moors in 1568, little remained of its ancient distinc-tion. Little too remains of the Alcazaba, except a few Moorish gates, but the site has been restored to a lovely series of terraced gardens (*open Mon–Sat 10–1 and 6–8*). At the top is an **Archaeological Museum** (*open 9.30–1.30 and 5–8 summer, 10–1 and 4–7 winter, mornings only on Sat and Sun*), containing relics from the Phoenician necropolis found on the site and lists of Moorish architectural decoration salvaged from the ruins. The top of the Alcazaba also affords fine views over Málaga. There is a half-ruined **Roman theatre**, recently excavated, on the lower slopes of the hill, and from the Alcazaba you may climb a little more to the **Gibralfaro** (*open 9–9*), the ruined Moorish castle that dominates the city.

Back on the Paseo, note the chunky Art-Nouveau **Ayuntamiento** (city hall), one of the more unusual buildings in Málaga. On the opposite side of the Alcazaba, is the **Museo de Bellas Artes**, Calle San Agustín 8 (*open 10–1.30 and 5–8, summer; 10–1 and 4–7, winter; closed Sun afternoon and Mon*), in a restored 16th-century palace. It's worth a look for some good medieval polychrome icons, two strange paintings by Luis de Morales (*c.* 1580) and a small collection of Picassos on the first floor. Picasso was a native of Málaga, though he left it at the age of 14 and never returned. Much of the museum is given over to the works of other late 19th-century *malagueño* painters who made up in eccentricity what they lacked in genius; one, Muñoz Degrain, was Picasso's first teacher. Also present are works of Zurbarán, Murillo and Ribera.

Málaga's **cathedral** is a few blocks away on Calle Molina Lario. It's an ugly, unfinished 16th-century work, immense and mouldering. Known as *La Manquita* (the one-armed lady), the only interesting feature is the faded, gaudy façade of the sacristy, left over from the earlier Isabelline Gothic church that once stood here. The **Museo de Arte Sacro**, is open daily except Sundays (*10–1 and 4–7*). Next to the dry river bed, the **Museo de Artes Populares**, Pasillo de Santa Isabel 10 (*open 10–1 and 5–8 in summer, 4–7 in winter; closed Sun*), occupies a restored 17th-century inn with a collection of household bric-a-brac from days gone by. Picasso's birthplace, **Casa Natal Picasso**, which now incorporates the **Municipal Picasso Foundation**, Plaza de la Merced, ✆ (95) 221 5005 (*open Mon–Fri 11–2 and 5–8*) is open for visits and holds occasional exhibitions.

Andalucía's Oldest Inn: an Outlaws' Retreat in Axarquía

At a lonely junction at the tip of Axarquía stands Andalucía's oldest inn. Until quite recently, a relentless stream of cars and lorries thundered past this *venta* without ceasing, for this was the old highway between Málaga and Granada. But the modern age has been kind to Alfarnate: now the traffic climbs through the gorges of the Río Guadalmedina on a swish new *carretera* over to the west, and the *venta* stands alone.

The Antigua Venta has an unmistakably ancient feel about it. Only a little imagination is required to see stagecoaches, stamping horses and menacing *bandoleros*. The Venta has seen its share of action. On a wall outside, a plaque records the overnight 'stay', under armed guard, of Luis Candelas, the infamous *madrileño* bandit, en route to trial in Málaga. Another notorious visitor, the sadistic *bandolero* Jose María el Tempranillo, threw a tantrum when the waiter forgot to bring him a spoon. Tempranillo ordered all the other diners to eat their spoons—at gunpoint. And the fact they were made not of metal but wood was their only consolation.

The Venta is the stuff of legend yet, reassuringly, it remains at heart a solid, down-to-earth wayside inn. Alfonso XIII ate here, and so did Picasso, but these days you're as likely to find a farm labourer or goatherd drinking at the bar as a bunch of *malagueña* dignitaries or a middle-class *granadina* family. Still a rarity, however, are tourists. Perhaps they think there are still bandits in the region; perhaps the smoke-filled, murky interior of the Venta reminds them too much of home, and they think that time is better spent turning black under a fierce Andalucian sun. But one day, not far off, the tourists are bound to come. And when they do, you may be quite sure the Antigua Venta de Alfarnate will take them in its stride.

getting there

From Málaga and the Costa del Sol, take the N331 (*ronda de Málaga*), continuing north in the direction of Antequera. Take the exit right at Casabermeja, following the MA435 to Colmenar. Just before the village, turn left on to the C340 then right after 4km on to the MA115. The Venta will appear on your right after 15km, on the corner of the road to Alfarnate.

From the eastern Costa del Sol via Vélez-Málaga, Periana and Alfarnate, the Venta is at the western edge of the village.

From Granada, take the A92 towards Antequera, bypassing Loja and turning on to the GR115 at Riofrío. This road brings you directly to the Venta.

COSTA DEL SOL

La Antigua Venta de Alfarnate

Antigua Carretera Málaga–Granada Km513.8, 29194 Alfarnate (Málaga),
℃ (95) 275 9235. Open daily noon–11pm; booking advisable.
About 4000 pts.

The Antiga Venta dates from the 14th century, although much has been added and rebuilt. A sense of its long history strikes you almost palpably as you enter. It's the sort of place where you could quite easily imagine the Wife of Bath, or Spanish equivalent thereof— perhaps a *mujer de Alfarnate*—holding court at the bar with pearls of homespun wisdom, or where an Andalucian Tom Jones crashing through the ceiling from a bedroom on the floor above would scarcely raise an eyebrow.

Of the Venta's four dining rooms, the first as you enter—the one containing the bar—and the second, which adjoins it, are perhaps the most appealing. You will be seated by one of the large team of staff; they all seem to be members of the family of the owner, Fernando Nuño. First to arrive on the table is a basket of steaming *pan cateto*, a round loaf of country bread made from stone-ground, unbleached white flour. Because this bread doesn't keep—it has a shelf life of about six hours—and has to be baked at home, it's becoming increasingly rare in Spain where, like everywhere else, 'supermarket' bread reigns supreme; getting the real thing is always a treat.

La Antigua Venta de Alfarnate

Andalucía's Oldest Inn: an Outlaws' Retreat in Axarquía

When you have settled down and ordered some wine—the house wine is a medium-dry, white *vino seco de los montes*, a good natural progression from a sherry *aperitivo*—your waitress will return with menus. The list is short, and one dish particularly will catch your eye. It is called, quite simply, *migas*.

Migas is a speciality of the Antigua Venta. It translates roughly as 'breadcrumbs', but this hardly gives the full picture. Rather like porridge or popcorn, it can be eaten sweet or savoury. Here at the Venta, *migas* is

La Antigua Venta de Alfarnate

savoury, fried with garlic, pepper and salt pork and served either on its own or as an accompaniment to a plate of sausage and eggs. It's a comforting, unsophisticated, enormously satisfying sort of dish, one that is essentially homemade. Finding it on a restaurant menu is rare. It's a trencherman's dish too, with a tendency to blow up in the stomach, rendering you incapable of eating anything more. The Venta has a custom whereby, if you finish your bowl of *migas*, they'll bring you another free of charge. Finish the second bowl and, if he's in a good mood, Fernando will give you a prize of 5000 pts. You may live to regret it.

For the faint-hearted, there are alternatives. *Setas en morrete*, a tangy casserole of wild mushrooms, is an excellent choice. All kinds of fungi proliferate in the countryside around Alfarnate; try looking for them yourself after lunch. A dish from Las Alpujarras, *berenjeñas con miel de caña*, may sound somewhat unappetizing but tastes delicious: honeyed aubergines fried in a light batter. They melt on the tongue.

If you have not already sampled *migas* for your first course, you might want to have it for your second. A simple salad of lettuce, tomato and onion makes a good accompaniment. Meat lovers will do no better than *chuletas de cordero lechal*, eight tiny baby-lamb cutlets grilled on an open fire. For something more robust, try *pato de cerdo asado*, roast leg of pork—fleshy white meat with just a hint of pink, served with crackling, Axarquía-style.

The desserts at the Venta are unremarkable. Anyhow, if you've eaten *migas*, dessert will be the last thing on your agenda. Instead, select an *aguardiente* or a local *digestivo* such as *anis* and take it outside to drink in the sunshine. You can now spend a very enjoyable half-hour or so sipping your drink and trying to spot that most fascinating of creatures, the *cabra hispanica*, the long-horned Spanish goat. It lives in the Sierra de Jobo, the foothills of which begin across the road from the Venta. Seeing it scale the cliffs at a near verticle angle is positively surreal: you will wonder if you haven't had one *anis* too many.

Migas

Migas is the quintessential peasant dish, requiring little more than stale bread, some oil and a bit of bacon rind. However, as with most 'peasant' food, a little care can elevate it into something quite remarkable.

(Serves 4)

1 large loaf of white bread, whole or sliced, with crusts
3 tablespoons vegetable oil
1 teaspoon dried chillies
6 bacon rashers, cut into small pieces, or 4oz/100g salt pork, diced
1 red pepper, deseeded and diced
6 cloves of finely chopped garlic
paprika (optional)

Take the bread and dice it into very small cubes. Put the whole lot into a bowl and dampen with a sprinkling of water. Now cover with a teatowel and leave to stand for a couple of hours, to allow the bread to absorb the water. The bread should be damp, without being soggy.

In a large frying pan, heat the oil and, when it starts to smoke, add the chillies. After a few seconds add the bacon or salt pork and fry for two to three minutes, until it begins to colour. Add the red pepper and the chopped garlic. Allow to sizzle for a couple of minutes, then add the breadcrumbs, quickly frying them until they turn golden brown. Some cooks add a little paprika, or pimenton, *at this stage to colour the* migas *and give them a little extra kick. Serve.*

To make sweet migas, *prepare the bread in the same way, then fry in vegetable oil with sugar and cinnamon or a vanilla pod. Serve piping hot with a cup of strong coffee or hot chocolate.*

---

touring around

The Málaga hinterland and the **region of Axarquía** is handsome, historic and well worth exploring. The most that average tourists get to see of this great swathe of land is a 30-second glimpse from the air a few minutes after their holiday jet takes off from Málaga Airport.

This is big country: a region long associated with *bandoleros* enjoying the spoils of goods and produce being carried between the Costa del Sol and Granada. And it is savage country: the whole area served as a guerrilla encampment during the Civil War, fighting on against the *Guardia Civil* until well into the 1950s, when most of the rest of Spain had buckled down under Franco's repressive rule.

Nowadays Axarquía makes fine walking country. An abundance of wildlife, flora and fauna, with a smattering of pretty, whitewashed villages spaced at decent intervals, make it perfect for casual hikers as well as the professional rambler. Alfarnate is a good base for exploring Axarquía; and although the Venta no longer has rooms, it keeps a three-bedroom house in the village which it lets out for a modest sum.

On foot or on wheels, one of Axarquía's most spectacular views is from the **Pass of Zafarraya**. To reach it, continue on the MA115 past the Venta in the direction of Riofrío, turning right after 4km onto the GR100 in the direction of **Zafarraya**. Continue through the village, on to **Ventas de Zafarraya**. The word *venta*, by the way, simply means a sales outlet, often referring to roadside stalls selling local produce, but extending to eateries and inns. Now carry on over the pass heading south towards **Trapiche** and **Vélez-Málaga**. On your left you will pass the ruins of a fort and the deserted medieval village of **Zalia**. Legend has it that this Moorish village was attacked by vipers after a local priest had unsuccessfully attempted to convert the inhabitants to Christianity.

Some 3km before you reach **Viñuela**, just past the intersection where the C335 meets the C340, a small track off to the left takes you to **Alcaucín**. This is a beautiful village in a wonderful location on the slopes of the **Sierra de Tejeda**. It's a delightful place to wander around in the relative cool of a summer evening. The village has Moorish origins, but traces of its Moorish past are hard to find.

Now you have a choice. Rejoining the main road, you can head back north along the C340 to **Periana**, a fairly ordinary place but one whose claim to fame is the production of *anis*, the aniseed-flavoured spirit. Alternatively, continuing south on the C335 brings you first to the village of **Viñuela**, with its 16th-century church of **San José**. Then, 2km after **Trapiche**, 1km before you reach Vélez-Málaga, a fork to the right takes you on a winding track of 6km or so to the tongue-twisting village of Macharaviaya. But first of all along this track, on the banks of the River Vélez at **Benamocarra**, lie the remains of a small Roman town; and a sign directs you to the **Necropolis de Jardin** nearby, which dates remarkably from the 6th century BC. **Macharaviaya** boasts an important church, built in 1785 by one José Gálvez, the Marqués de Sonora. At the time, Gálvez was government minister for the Indies and his family played an important role in southern American history. Galveston, Texas, is named after him.

Vélez-Málaga (or simply Vélez, as this capital of Axarquía is commonly known) is one of Málaga province's most important towns. It's built-up and industrial, although the remains of the **Alcázar** (the Moorish fortified palace) are worth a visit, as is the well-preserved **Barrio de San Francisco**, an area built in the 16th and 17th centuries and boasting some fine noblemen's houses as well as the odd *mudéjar* palace with a distinctive mix of Moorish and medieval European architecture. The **House of Cervantes** was where the great writer lived when he worked as a tax-collector in Vélez.

Continuing 4km further south brings you back to the coast at **Torre del Mar**. From here, turn left for the resort of **Nerja** and the eastern Costa del Sol, or right for the slow haul back to **Málaga**, through some 15km of ribbon development, which can be softened to a large degree by the sight of the setting sun upon a gentian-blue Mediterranean.

¡Viva La Corrida!

La Espuela

Antiquaria: even to the Romans who named it, this was an ancient settlement. Its dolmens, 5000-year-old burial chambers built from rock, bear witness to its real antiquity. Modern-day Antequera is one of Andalucía's most underrated towns. At the four points of the compass, the great cities and tourist centres of the region call out: to the west, Sevilla; to the the north, Córdoba; to the east, Granada; and to the south, the Costa del Sol. Poor old Antequera doesn't seem to stand a chance.

But therein lies its appeal. For it's a totally Spanish place, blessed with enough work and light industry to keep its economy healthy and a culinary heritage which is very much alive and well. It's also got the best ice-cream parlours in all of southern Spain—no wonder the *antequeros* seem to walk out with a spring in their step.

When Madonna wanted to film a pop video in Ronda's famous bullring, the Plaza de Toros, in the spring of 1995, the Ayuntamiento (city hall) quoted her a price rumoured to be in excess of £1 million. Pounds, not dollars, mark you. No mug, the American songstress: she and her entourage upped and went, heading east to Antequera. The town hall was only too pleased to hire out *their* bullring to the star—at less than one per cent of Ronda's asking price. Antequera is generous, fair and fun-loving: after all, a town that played host to Julius Caesar must have a well-developed sense of *noblesse oblige*.

Being the setting of Madonna's video is not the Plaza de Toros' only claim to fame. Beneath the bullring's front seats lies La Espuela, the only proper restaurant located in a bullring in Spain. The location is irresistible and the atmosphere is superb—rising to fever pitch on *corrida* days when you practically have to kill to get a table. On most days, however, it's a relaxed sort of place, where they'll welcome you to lunch any time between noon and 5pm. This is a restaurant for meat-lovers, for what more appropriate place to tuck into a dish of *rabo de toro*, La Espuela's oxtail speciality, than in a bullring? Definitely not for the squeamish. Or is it perhaps just a case of life imitating art?

To complete your day out, you can stroll around the centre of Antequera, visit the prehistoric dolmens on the outskirts of the town, and tour the spectacular sierras between Antequera and Málaga.

getting there

Antequera lies at the heart of southern Spain's newest road system. Reach it from Sevilla or Granada on the A92, or from Málaga on the N331. From Córdoba, however, the route is still slow and tedious. Upgrading and bypasses are planned for various points along the N331 but expect no major improvements until 1998. Meanwhile the best route between Córdoba and Antequera is as

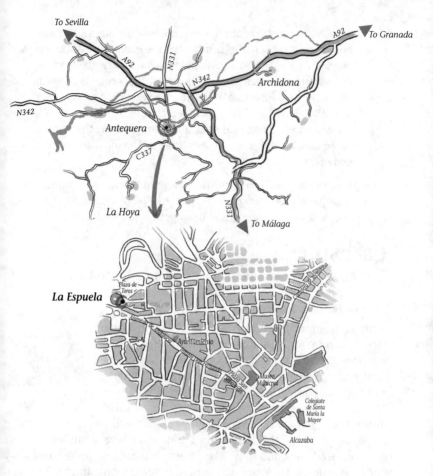

follows: take the N1V/E5 south out of Córdoba in the direction of Sevilla, turning south after 15km on to the N331 (signposted Málaga). After 33km, at Aguilar, take the C329 to Puente-Genil, join the C328 to bypass the town and take you in the direction of Estepa. Join the A92 *autopista* just east of Estepa, in the direction of Antequera and Málaga. This rather convoluted route will save you a great deal of frustration on the congested N331.

Once in the town, you will need to find the Plaza de Toros, located below the bus station on the western perimeter. The road in from

Sevilla, and from Córdoba too, if you follow the directions above, brings you directly to this point, along the Alameda de Andalucía. From Granada, Málaga and Archidona, you'll enter the town via the Carretera de Archidona; follow the town's one-way system, and with any luck find yourself eventually in the Plaza San Sebastián. From here, take Calle Infante Don Fernando, passing the Ayuntamiento on your right, and continue along the Alameda de Andalucía until you see the bullring by the roundabout at the end of the street.

Don't worry if you get lost navigating your way through Antequera's confusing streets: just ask for the Plaza de Toros. Everyone knows it, and it's well signposted into the bargain.

La Espuela

La Espuela, Paseo Maria Cristina s/n, Plaza de Toros, 29200 Antequera (Málaga), © (95) 270 2676, ◉ (95) 284 2633. Open daily noon–5pm 8.30–11.30pm. 3000 pts.

With two terraces, a garden and tables on the street, there's no prize for guessing where locals prefer to eat in warm weather. That's right, you've got it: inside—in the faintly gloomy surroundings of the restaurant proper, with its dark wood and earthenware decorations. Andalucians have an antipathy to strong sunlight. Inside, though, more than out, you'll be able to soak up the atmosphere of this restaurant's unique setting. Proprietor, director, head cook and most likely bottle-washer too, Jesús López Carillo has devised a menu which pays tribute to Antequera's fine culinary tradition.

The tables are nicely spaced, wide and comfortable. To start, order a bottle of *Montelobo*, a local white from Mollina which is drier than most of Málaga's wines but not bone dry: it makes an excellent *aperitivo*. First-time visitors to Antequera should now move straight into the town's most famous dish, *porra antequerana*. This is actually a dip, though when thin enough it can be eaten as a soup. Tomato, garlic, green pepper, ham and tuna, blended to a creamy consistency, are the principal players; it could make a good shared hors-d'œuvre to accompany your *aperitivo*. *Pimientos de Antequera rellenos de sepia y gambas* is another choice starter: fat, sweet, red peppers stuffed with squid and prawns.

The wine list is enticing, short but thoughtfully chosen, particularly the reds: with very little mark-up, this might be the place to splash out. The Valdepeñas *Viña Alvali* '86 is a big wine with a long finish; *Faustino I Gran Reserva*, a top-of-the-line blackish-red wine from Rioja Alavesa, weighs in at a hefty 5500 pts, but is worth every peseta; and you'll even fare well with *Otoñal*, a well-made, reliable young Rioja for next to nothing at 900 pts.

All these wines will go very well indeed with La Espuela's signature dish, *rabo de toro estofado con miel de romero*, an oxtail stew with rosemary-flavoured honey. This is a powerful dish, rich, and enormously filling. The tender meat falls off the bone, and the honey, produced by local bees from winter-flowering rosemary, lends it fragrance and sweetness. After a *corrida*, incidentally, you'll be sampling this dish made with actual bulls' tails; though to be honest, you'd be hard pressed to tell an ox's and a bull's tail apart.

Other main courses which La Espuela prepares well are *conejo a la cazadora*, a 'hunter's' rabbit with almonds; a dish borrowed from Toledo, *faisan al toledano*, pheasant with beer and onions; or, if fish is your preference, *pez espada al Carpe Diem con pasas*, a very subtle dish of swordfish with raisins cooked in Carpe Diem, a sweet local wine from Mollina.

If the waiter is eager to press you to have dessert, it's only because he's proud of what's on offer. Instead you might try another bottle of wine—this restaurant's last orders for lunch are at 5pm, so they won't be in any hurry to get rid of you.

But dessert is worth ordering eventually. No freezer cabinet here: everything is truly *casera*, or homemade, which one quickly comes to realize is a luxury in Andalucía. You'll do no better than *bienmesabe antequerano*, a soft marzipan cake with sugar and the ubiquitous almond; that is, of course, unless you dislike marzipan, in which case you could try instead the exotic *compota de batata con miel de cana*, a compote of sweet potatoes with molasses, presumably a post-Cortez dish that must have its origins in the New World.

After lunch, wander into the bullring; you might catch some local matador wannabes flourishing their capes—or maybe you're a wannabe yourself. At any rate, no one will stop you daydreaming.

Espuela means a spur, the horsy emblem of this unusual restaurant. But it has another meaning too: 'one for the road'. With coffee you could have your *espuela*, perhaps a throat-burning *aguardiente* from nearby Rute.

Rabo de Buey Estofado con Miel de Romero

Ovens are a relatively new feature in the Andalucian kitchen. This dish, an oxtail stew with honey, is cooked entirely on top of the stove. You'll need a large flameproof casserole to do it, either earthenware or enamel—and with a tight-fitting lid.

Rosemary-flavoured honey can be found in health-food shops and good delicatessens. If you can't find it, don't worry: the dish will work perfectly well with any shop-bought, clear honey if a couple of sprigs of rosemary are popped into the casserole along with the honey.

(Serves 6)

3kg/7lbs oxtails
4 tablespoons olive oil
4 garlic cloves, cut in half
1 large onion, chopped
6 bacon rashers or 150g/5oz panacetta, diced
2 carrots, chopped
200ml/7fl oz sherry or brandy
pinch of mace
1 teaspoon dried chillies
I tablespoon paprika
12 green peppercorns, crushed
450g/1lb tin peeled plum tomatoes

900ml/1½ pints stock
250g/9oz tin red kidney beans
250g/9oz tin haricot beans
2 tablespoons rosemary honey
salt and pepper

First, wash and pat dry the oxtails. Trim off any excess fat and cut into joints, about 10cm (4in) long. Heat the oil in the casserole, add the garlic, and when it is very hot, put in the oxtails. Turn them a few times, just enough to lose their raw colour, and remove them. Now, put in the chopped onion and sauté for two to three minutes until it's translucent but without allowing it to colour; then add the bacon (or pancetta) and the carrots and continue to sauté for a further two minutes. When the flavours have begun to combine, return the oxtails to the pan and, off the heat, add the sherry (or brandy). Now turn the heat to high and cook for a couple of minutes or until reduced by half.

Add the mace, chillies, peppercorns and paprika and give it all a good stir before adding the tomatoes.

Meanwhile, in a separate saucepan, heat the stock and blend in the honey. Once the honey has been absorbed, add enough of the liquid to the casserole to cover everything completely, reserving the rest. Bring all the ingredients to the boil, before turning down the heat to a very gentle simmer—you should see no more than the occasional bubble.

Cover the casserole and cook for two hours; then add the kidney and haricot beans. Cook slowly for a further hour until the beans are soft and the meat comes away easily from the bone. Every now and then, check the cooking liquid and, if it has reduced, add more of the stock. The oxtails should remain barely covered, but not drowned, throughout.

touring around

In the centre of **Antequera** there's an impressive ensemble of 16th- to 18th-century buildings. The 17th-century Nerja Palace houses the **Museo Municipal** (*open Tues–Fri 10–1.30; Sat 10–1; adm*), with religious works including a wonderful St Francis by Alonso Cano and the *Efebo de Antequera*—a remarkable Roman bronze figure of a boy.

Up the Cuesta Zapateros, at the top of the hill, is the 16th-century **Arco de los Gigantes**, meant as a sort of triumphal arch for the seldom-victorious Philip II, and incorporating ancient fragments; next to it, the ruins of a Moorish fortress, the **Alcazaba**. Nearby is the heavily ornamented 16th-century church of **Santa María La Mayor**, with a magnificent 12m Baroque carved wood altarpiece. Attached to the church is an art restoration centre, teaching stonemasonry, woodwork and ironwork.

One of the most rewarding sights to see in Antequera, however, is its three **dolmens**, (*usually open Tues–Fri 10–1.30 and 3.30–6; Sat and Sun 10–1.30; adm*), 1km from the centre of Antequera on the old Granada road—they're well signposted. Europe's answer to the tombs of the pharaohs, these sepulchral chambers, built from great slabs of unhewn rock, contain an anteroom for the possessions of the dead, as well as the burial room itself. They're not as impressive as the *talayots* and *taulas* of the island of Menorca, but there's nothing else like them in mainland Spain. Le Corbusier came here in the 1950s, as he said 'to pay homage to my predecessors'. The **Cueva de Menga**, which dates from around 2500 BC, is the simplest of the three, although its proportions are huge—it measures 23m by 7.5m. About 50m away is the **Cueva de Viera**, which was discovered in 1905. Reached by a 20m corridor, the chamber itself is much smaller than that of Menga. The **Cueva de Romeral** is the most recent of the three; it was discovered at about the same time as Viera, but is quite different to its two neighbours, with its domed ceiling and grotto-like walls made of mud and small stones. Romeral is located 4km from Menga and Viera; to reach it from the other *cuevas*, continue along the same road (in the direction of Granada) for 2km, watching out for a sugar factory. Romeral is behind it. Cross the railway line and follow the sign which leads you off the main road to the left.

A word about **sunsets**. If your lunch at La Espuela lingers on, and evening finds you still in town, try climbing the Cuesta de los Rojas to the Alcazaba. From the public gardens within the ruined fortress, the views over the town to the **Peña de los Enamorados** are truly spectacular. This *peña* is a rock like no other; a giant, twisted volcanic mass soaring into the sky, named for two lovers who were said to have thrown themselves from the rock when their parents forbade them to marry. Then turn around to look behind you to the west and watch the fireball sun sink into the hills. It's an experience you won't forget.

Some 15km east of Antequera on the N342 is **Archidona**. The town overlooks acres of olive trees, but its main feature is the unique, octagonal Plaza Mayor, the **Ochavada**. Built in 1780–86 by Francisco Astorga and Antonio González, it is one of the loveliest plazas in Andalucía. Nearby **Loja** had a 9th-century **alcazaba**, and its 16th-century church of **San Gabriel** has a cupola attributed to Diego de Siloé, who began the cathedrals in Granada and Úbeda.

The **sierras** between Antequera and Málaga contain some of the most remote villages of the region and offer some spectacular scenery—almond trees, cactus, olive groves and mountains that drop steeply away to the silver ribbon of a stream down below. A natural park has been laid out around the rock formations at **El Torcal**, a tall but hikeable mountain with unusual, eroded red limestone crags around it. Several paths are marked out. The nearest town is **Villanueva de la Concepción**. Here you should take the MA424 and travel south for about 17km. You will be rewarded with **Almogía**, presenting a dramatic spectacle overlooking a high ridge. From 15 to 18 August this place comes to life with dancing in the streets in celebration of San Roque and San Sebastián. The best views are from the ruined tower.

A more roundabout route south from Antequera will take you to the town of **Alora**. Originally a Roman settlement and one of the last towns to be held by the Moors, it is mainly of interest now as the point where you should turn northwest towards one of Andalucía's natural wonders. **El Chorro gorge**, in the deep rugged canyon of the Río Guadalhorce, has sheer walls of limestone tossed about at crazy angles. Thrill-seekers can circumnavigate it on an old concrete catwalk called **El Camino del Rey**, which is gradually crumbling into a ruin; it's amazing they still keep it open. It's definitely worth the walk if you're nimble and don't suffer from vertigo.

If you have time to explore this region, seek out the church of **Bobastro**. Just west of El Chorro, it's a twisty drive for a couple of kilometres after turning off the little Alora–Ardales road. Bobastro is a 9th-century basilica cut out of bare rock that supposedly contains the tomb of Ibn Hafsun, the (possibly) Christian emir who founded a short-lived independent state in the mountains around AD 880. Some remains of the city and fortress he built can be seen on the neighbouring heights. The nearby lakes were created as part of a big government hydroelectric scheme, but their shores, surrounded by gentle hills, make an ideal place to spend a lazy afternoon.

From Bobastro follow the road to **Ardales** and **Carratraca**. Carratraca has been a spa town from Greek and Roman times, but its heyday was in the 19th and early 20th centuries. Visitors included Byron, Dumas, Rilke and Napoleon II's wife, the Empress Eugénie, who gadded about everywhere in Europe and lived to the ripe old age of 94. The baths have been restored and can be visited by cure-seekers from June to October. The town is also famous for its Passion play. As part of their *Semana Santa* celebrations, 140 of the villagers perform *El Paso* in the bullring. From here the road twists its way back to Alora.

At the Front Door of Las Alpujarras

Despite the heinous crimes laid at his door—the murder of his sister and her two children, for one thing—one can't help sympathizing with Boabdil, last Arab king of Moorish Granada. Having just handed over the keys of the city to the conquering Christians, he left Granada to head south and, at the spot now called Suspiro del Moro (the Sigh of the Moor), he turned round to look back at his beloved Granada and bemoan his fate. His mother, his staunchest supporter and childhood defender against a tyrannical and savage father, could offer no words of comfort. 'You do well to weep like a woman,' she told him, 'for what you could not defend as a man.'

When you've lived all your life in the Alhambra, it's understandably hard to know where to go next. After all,

nowhere's going to carry quite the same clout. But Boabdil knew a thing or two, and his negotiated surrender of Granada gave him the fiefdom of Las Alpujarras, the mountainous lands which run, more or less diagonally, between Granada and the coast at Almería.

You'll soon see its appeal. This 'Switzerland of Spain', as Richard Ford called it back in the 1840s, is fertile country. Olives, almonds, fruits of all kinds—even bananas—grow on Las Alpujarras' slopes. In Trevélez, Spain's highest village, the celebrated mountain ham is sharp and sweet. But while Las Alpujarras have an ancient and distinctive cuisine, tracking down good examples of it is hard work indeed. In *South from Granada*, written in the 1920s, Gerald Brenan describes an inn where 'the only food consisted of an oily rice cooked with the nastiest of dried cod'. Some guide books gush excitedly about baby kid, Alpujarras stew, black pudding and pickled partridge but, more often than not, this mountain fare simply doesn't taste as good as it sounds.

Not so at El Molino. In Dúrcal, near Las Alpujarras' 'front door' at Lanjarón, Javier Carrillo Díaz has created a gastronomy centre which celebrates Andalucía's cuisine, and the food of Las Alpujarras in particular. The setting, in a clearing in a valley of the Río Dúrcal, is pure enchantment. The food, a studied presentation of all that's best from Las Alpujarras, is *precioso*. This is a gem which will truly delight you.

The hapless Boabdil would definitely have approved.

getting there

Dúrcal is easy to find; El Molino is not.

From the Alhambra, central Granada and directions from the north, follow signs for the *Ronda de Granada* (ring-road), confusingly numbered N323 and E902, and join it travelling south in the direction of Motril. (Don't join the spur road called *Ronda del Sur*—

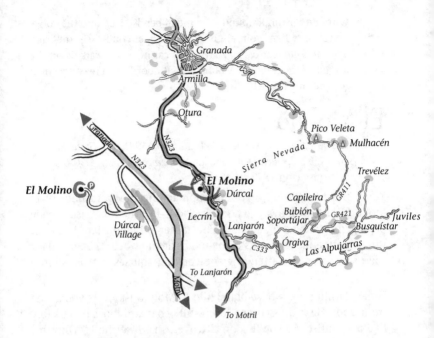

it's Motril and Motril only you must follow signs for). This road, which is proper *autovía* until the city limits, takes you past the exits for Armilla and Otura before you reach the right-hand turn-off for Dúrcal, about 30km south of central Granada. Drive around the spectacular gorge and up into the village.

If you're coming from the eastern Costa del Sol or the Costa de Almería along the coastal N340, turn off at Salobreña (3km west of Motril—no need to go into Motril) onto the N323/E902, sign-posted Granada. Turn off at the first sign to Dúrcal (about 35km from the coast) and drive into the village.

Once in the village of Dúrcal, the road to El Molino is indicated by a small sign (visible from either direction) at the Granada (northern) end of the main street—*El Molino 500 metros*. Follow the street indicated, taking the left hand (lower) fork where the road divides. Continue down the hill, and don't be put off when the road runs out and becomes a stone path. Just take it slowly.

Carry on downhill, round a couple of bends, deep into the gorge, and just when you're giving up hope you'll see the sign *aparcamiento* (car park). Leave your car here and walk down the last bit of the hill to El Molino's front door. If you're early, you'll have to ring the bell.

El Molino

Camino de las Fuentes, Paraje de la Isla s/n, 18650 Dúrcal (Granada),
© (95) 878 0247. Open Thurs, Fri, Sat, Sun, lunchtime only, 1.30–3.30.
Menú degustación *3800 pts.*

You'll feel like Hansel or Gretel approaching the front door of El Molino. It's tucked away in a forest glade—but the house isn't made of gingerbread: it's a solid, handsome, rather forbidding farmhouse on three floors, and some of its many rooms are now being converted for the use of students attending the cooking courses that El Molino regularly holds.

Javier Carillo Díaz, whose brainchild El Molino is, greets you at the front door. He is dressed in a long white coat and looks remarkably like a scientist. As you'll soon discover, in a way he is. Only his 'science' is that of food, and its preparation in ways both old and new.

Inside, the ground floor is given over to a display of old kitchen equipment and utensils: giant sieves, treadmills and spatulas dating back 200 years. On a winter's day, despite the warm atmosphere, it can be pretty cold inside, and the

El Molino

aperitivo of Manzanilla sherry which Javier pours you is very welcome. So are the little appetizers that go with it: some spicy sausages with cumin or perhaps slivers of *jamón* from Trevélez, Las Alpujarras' celebrated centre of ham.

After showing you around the two downstairs kitchens—a fascinating combination of ancient and modern apparatus and an Aga-type range that many thirtysomethings would kill for—it's upstairs to one of El Molino's dining rooms for lunch. Each is lovely: the summer room, light and airy with lots of pretty antique lace; and the winter room, oak-beamed, ingle-nooky and deliciously warm. There's no menu as such but, once seated at your table, Javier will tell you what's on offer and talk through particular dishes with you.

The *menú degustación* is a good introduction to the *cocina arabigo andaluza*, or Arab Andaluz cuisine, that is El Molino's hallmark. This menu changes daily but might run as follows. To start, some pickled red cabbage served with three kinds of bread, a doughy white roll, a nutty brown one and a *cateta* or rustic bread; then *sopa de almendras*, a creamy soup of chopped almonds, mint and cumin, and a staple Arab dish of Las Alpujarras. Wines, incidentally, are included in the price and are chosen to complement the style of the day's dishes. The very young, green *Blanco Afrutado*, from the Doñana region of Huelva province, tastes fuller, fatter and fruitier than it has any right to; it makes a magical combination with the almond soup. The next course might be a trout from the Guadalfeo river which runs through Las Alpujarras, caught most likely only hours before and lightly poached in wine and garlic.

Next a little intermission, and with it the appearance of a dish of bright yellow *calabacín*—a rich, juicy marrow lightly steamed and drizzled with fruity, green olive oil. At this point you might switch to *vino tinto*, a treacly 1991 *Cortijo de Balsillas* from Baza, to the north of Granada. It's a local wine which can compete with better-known houses in both its quality and style.

olive oil

In common with most of Andalucía, where meal times are always later than you might expect, El Molino doesn't really get into its stride until about 3pm. Around this time the bulk of the mainly Spanish guests arrive, just as you're tucking into the fifth item on the *menú*, *filete de ternera*—strips of beef in a subtle sauce of puréed artichoke heart. The small, well-disciplined army of waiting staff seems endlessly to ferry small and delectable dishes to the newly arrived guests and every so often Javier stops by the table to make sure everything is in order and that you are enjoying your meal. He is justifiably proud of the unique establishment he's created, where he balances the science of his *investigaciónes gastronómicas* with the art of hospitality.

A selection of three desserts arrives. *Bizcocho al limón*, a lemon sponge cake, is the least exotic of the three, but the other two, a bread pudding in milk, and honeyed figs in an almond sauce, are excellent. *Café andaluz*, a malted coffee Arabic in origin, follows—served with a *madeleine*, American muffin or, most correctly, *pan de bizcocho*, sponge cake.

Even the bill at El Molino is a pleasure. Each item is written out in a fine, old-fashioned hand (a good record of a very special lunch) and Javier brings it to the table with a discretion bordering on diffidence. At an establishment of this class, money just isn't talked about.

Sopa de Almendras con Hierbabuena

This nourishing almond-and-mint soup is quick and easy to make.

(Serves 8)

6 tablespoons olive oil
225g/8oz peeled almonds
2 garlic cloves, peeled
2.25 litres/4 pints chicken stock
8 slices brown bread
10 leaves fresh mint
sea salt and freshly ground pepper
1 teaspoon ground cumin

In a large saucepan, heat half the oil and gently fry the almonds for two to three minutes with one of the cloves of garlic. Add the chicken stock, then whizz the whole lot in a blender until smooth.

Now return the soup to the saucepan and heat gently for 20 minutes, allowing the almond flavour to emerge. While it's cooking, remove the crusts from the sliced bread and cut into triangles. Heat the remaining three tablespoons of olive oil in a pan with the second clove of garlic, then lightly fry the bread on both sides until it turns golden brown.

Now add the mint leaves to the soup, season with sea salt, pepper and cumin, and serve in individual wide bowls with a couple of triangles of fried bread on the top.

touring around

Dúrcal itself is a pleasant village with a modern but agreeable church and main square, Plaza de España. The number of new houses being built around the village bears witness to the area's prosperity: this is commuter-land for Granada.

Six km to the south, the village of **Lecrín** held the burial ground of the kings of Granada. It is generally thought that the last burial to take place here was that of Moraima, Boabdil's wife. There's nothing much to see here these days, except Abu al-Hassan's ruined castle—he was Boabdil's dad.

Continue south for a couple of kilometres on the N323, then take the C333 to **Lanjarón**. This spa town in the western Alpujarras is the region's front door—and certainly the easiest approach. Spain's most visited spa is a delightful town, famous for its medicinal waters and the eponymous flat mineral water it produces. Lanjarón had a bloody history when the Catholic Kings tried to take it from the Moors who had been granted refuge there: 300 Moslems died in 1500 when their mosque was blown up by a rampaging Fernando and later, in 1568, 20 Christians were burnt alive when Aben Farag, sheriff of Las Alpujarras, razed the town to the ground.

Five hundred years after Boabdil headed into Las Alpujarras, the British writer Gerald Brenan immortalized the region in *South from Granada*. Written between 1920 and 1930, this classic work records

Brenan's life in Yengen, a typical flat-roofed village at the Almería end of the Alpujarras. Many have since followed in Brenan's footsteps: English, Dutch, Germans and Scandinavians have come this way, a pair of hiking boots in one hand and *South from Granada* in the other—never to return home.

You'll meet many of them in the bars of **Órgiva**, next stop after Lanjarón and Las Alpujarras' biggest village. The **palace** of the Counts of Sástago (now containing shops), and the 16th-century parish **church** with a carving by Martínez Montañés, are well worth visiting, but one of Órgiva's highlights is its **Thursday market**. Arts, crafts, rugs, pottery, tupperware—along with a thousand items you couldn't possibly live without, such as Snow White and the Seven Dwarfs lavatory brushes—are on sale here, the whole spectacle made yet more colourful by armies of Brenan groupies looking like they've lost their way to Woodstock.

From Órgiva, you'll have a choice of keeping to the main road for Ugíjar, or heading north through the highest and loveliest part of the region, with typical white villages climbing the hillsides under terraced fields. **Soportújar**, the first, has one of Las Alpujarras' surviving primeval oak groves behind it. Next comes **Pampaneira**, a pretty little town of cobbled streets and flowers. In the Plaza Mayor there's a museum dedicated to the customs and costumes of Las Alpujarras. **Bubión** is a Berber-style village with an old textile mill, but it's becoming more touristy by the minute, a situation exacerbated by the well-intentioned but jarring *Villa Turística* hotel complex.

All these villages are within sight of each other on a short detour along the edge of the beautiful (but walkable) ravine called **Barranco de Poqueira**. **Capileira**, the last village on the mountain pass over Mulhacén and Veleta, sees more tourists than most. North from here the road (the GR411) takes you up across the Sierra Nevada and eventually to Granada. In winter this pass is snowbound, and even in summer you need to take extra care—it's steep and dangerous with precipitous drops down the ravines. However, the beautiful scenery makes the risks worthwhile. Alternatively, continue on the GR421 to **Pitres**, centre of a Hispano-Japanese joint venture that produces and exports handcrafted ballet shoes—of all things.

The road carries on through the villages of **Pórtugos** and **Busquístar** before arriving in **Trevélez**, on the slopes of Mulhacén. Trevélez claims to be the highest village in Europe. It's also famous in Andalucía for its snow-cured hams—and very good they are too. No matter what  time of day you stop here, take a walk around the village and call in at **La Fragua**, a modest inn above the main square and along the street (it's well signposted), for a glass of *fino* and a *ración* of ham. From here the road slopes back downwards to Juviles and **Bérchules**, one of the villages where the traditional art of carpet weaving has been maintained since Moorish times. **Yegen**, some 10km further, was of course Brenan's home. It doesn't look much from the main road, but down in the village you can see Brenan's house (indicated by a plaque) and check out this rural hamlet which so inspired him. After that come more intensively farmed areas on the lower slopes, with oranges, vineyards and almonds. You can either hit Ugíjar and the main roads to the coast and Almería, or detour to the seldom-visited villages of **Mairena** and **Laroles** on the slopes of La Ragua, one of the last high peaks of the Sierra Nevada. Further east, through countryside that rapidly changes from healthy green to dry brown, the village of **Fondón** is of particular interest; an Australian architect, Donald Grey, and his Spanish partner, José Antonio Garvayo, have set up a school here to teach the traditional crafts of ironwork, carpentry and tile- and brick-making, so most of the buildings have been restored and Fondón is now a model village.

Down here, Granada feels like a lifetime away; how Boabdil must have yearned for it. At any rate, he didn't last long in Las Alpujarras. A year after settling in, his presence became insupportable and he was packed off again. Like an old man returning to the place of his birth, his destination this time was perhaps more fitting: Fez, in Morocco.

'Manna and Dates, in Argosy Transferred'

Almería, the most easterly province of Andalucía, is a curious place. A thousand years ago, in the provincial capital also called Almería, Abd al-Rahman, caliph of Córdoba, built a fortress and from its ramparts surveyed what was then his caliphate's most important port, routinely trading with Africa and the Orient.

Almería was to become the capital of a kingdom which stretched across a vast area of southern Spain. Caravans loaded with raw silk would make their way to the city, across the southern flank of Las Alpujarras, where silkworms feasted on white mulberry trees to produce the finest thread in Europe, surpassing that of Florence and Nantes both in quality and

courtyard of Hotel Balneario

production. Ten thousand looms in the city turned out silk, cotton and linen damask, and Almería waxed rich.

After the fall of the caliphate in 1031, Almería rivalled Sevilla and Córdoba as a cultural and industrial centre, and became the country's most important port. But things could not last; in 1490 the city fell to Fernando, and the Moors were expelled. The province of Almería went into terminal decline. Half a millennium on and you feel it still—Andalucía's poor relation, struggling to find a modern identity. Take the city of Almería itself: it's a pleasant enough place, but it lacks a soul. Only up on the ramparts of the alcazaba can you detect a heartbeat still—or down in the port, where a vast container-ship, loaded to the gills and ready to sail, sounds its foghorns and starts for Melilla, its sister-port across the water in Africa.

But head north or west from the city—where the fertile, coastal plain dries up, stretching for ever into a rocky, lunar landscape—and it's a different story. Here you'll feel the drum-roll of an Arab land. It is here, in the arid emptiness of this parched, unyielding region, that this mood steals upon you, more than anywhere in all Andalucía. The insouciant angle of a date palm, set against a deep blue sky, a goatherd walking with his goats, body, hands and face wrapped up against a scorching sun—not Spanish, these, but ancient, Arab images which tone and punctuate the landscape.

At Pechina, a mere 7km from the city, a signpost directs you up into the turquoise haze of the sierras. Climb a few kilometres more and you come to Baños, a microdot on Andalucía's vast map, a village so small it has no street other than the one that brings you from Pechina.

This minuscule village is a spa, or so it calls itself. 'Oasis' would describe it better, with its lush palm groves and abundant water in a place which is essentially dry. Here you will feel you've left Europe far behind, and travelled deep into the heart of Africa. (For a note on using the spa facilities and staying at Hotel Balneario, *see* 'touring around', p.45).

getting there

From Granada, Guadix and the northern Alpujarras, the N324 and the C3326 will bring you to the junction with the N340. From here, turn right onto the N340 in the direction of Almería to Benahadux, then, after 2km turn left to Pechina. At Pechina, turn left towards Rioja, then, after 300m, follow the next right turn, signposted to Baños de S. Alhamilla. In Baños, the hotel is the first building on your left. For the hotel entrance, carry on until the end of the 'street', turn left, and left again.

From Almería, take the N340, following signs to Guadix and Granada. After 7km, at the sign for Chuche, turn right, continuing on to Pechina. From Pechina, continue as described above.

Balneario de Sierra Alhamilla

Baños de Sierra Alhamilla, 04250 Pechina (Almería), ☎ and ✉ (95) 031 7413. Open daily 1.30–3.30 and 8.30–11; booking essential. Set menu from 1850 pts.

Hotel Balneario baths

What is it doing here? Who comes here? These will be your first incredulous questions as you set foot inside the Balneario, a magnificent 18th-century palace now up-and-running as a hotel after eight years of dedicated and very costly restoration.

You are the answer to these questions. For despite—or perhaps because of—Baños' splendid isolation, romantics and people with an eye for beauty will always make their way here. Not that it's ever busy: this is a rural retreat par excellence, where you'll often find yourself alone, with only plaintive birdsong and the chattering fountain in the central courtyard for company.

As befits a spa hotel, the food here is light, but in no way spartanly *diététique*. However, the natural produce of Almería, Andalucía's market garden, make this an obvious place for healthy eating.

The Moorish-inspired dining room has plasterwork so elaborate one wonders if it mightn't make its cousins in Granada just a trifle jealous. In spring and autumn, when the air is neither too hot nor too cool, the huge oak door at the end of the dining room is left open and gives on to a terrace, with unequalled views across the sierra to the coast. Here, in this perfect setting, the talented young chef serves up a fish soup like no other. No rich stock or heavy seasoning, but a simple fish bouillon made with the freshest of *mariscos*: it's almost Japanese in its lightness of touch.

Wonderfully fresh escarole lettuce is the main ingredient in a *sopa de lechuga*, a lettuce soup, or *fideos con escarol*, thin noodles with escarole and garlic. For a main course, choose perhaps *escabeche de sardinas*, sardines pickled in aromatic vinegar, or an *arroz a banda*, Almería's meaty *paella* made with white fish, saffron and red peppers (these 'fruity' vegetables are Almería's pride and joy).

There's a good choice of local wines to wash it down with: Purchena's *Moscatel* for one, and don't be shy about asking for ice-cubes if you need to cool it down. This wine needs to be drunk very cold.

Desserts in Almería mean fruit; in the winter months, big, sweet oranges from Benahadux, fat, white grapes from Ojanes or *datiles cocidos*, sugared dates, which the Moors first brought here a thousand years ago—manna transferred in the argosies of Keats' imagination.

Datiles Cocidos

The date is an exotic fruit which makes one think instinctively of the Middle East—Turkey, Lebanon, Arabia and of course Israel, where fresh dates picked straight from the palm-tree have a yellow, unwrinkled appearance.

Though the date is less prolific in southern Spain, it's fleshy and the flavour is excellent. This recipe for sugared dates is a match made in heaven for the Spaniard and his sweet tooth.

These amounts will serve four people for dessert, or eight to ten as a sweetmeat or petit four.

500g/1lb 2oz fresh dates
120g/4oz caster sugar

Put the dates in a saucepan with just enough water to cover them. Bring to the boil and simmer very gently, uncovered, for 30 minutes. Drain off the water, and allow the dates to dry; then dredge them in the caster sugar and arrange on a dish.

For a luxurious petit four, *remove the stone and replace it with a blanched almond, a sliver of* turrón *(nougat), or a chocolate coffee-bean.*

touring around

The **Hotel Balneario** incorporates a natural spa which is open to non-residents and where you can enjoy all manner of treatments. If possible, arrange your day to arrive at Baños in the early morning, or plan to stay here the night before (most treatments take place in the morning). The extremely comfortable rooms, built around an elegant gallery above the central courtyard, start at a very reasonable 6500 pts. Bathed, massaged, primped, plucked and cosseted, you'll feel like a new person by lunch time.

Spa aficionados might like to know that the Sierra Alhamilla spa waters contain bicarbonate, sulphur, chlorides, sodium and magnesium. Treatments include thermal baths, underwater massage, and inhalations; there are specialized treatments for arthritis, neurological complaints, asthma, bronchitis, dyspepsia, kidney problems, stress and obesity—to name but a few. There's a full range of beauty treatments too, as well as a supervised gym. Most treatments should be booked in advance by telephoning ✆ (95) 031 7413.

Almería, the provincial capital of Almería province, has been a genial, dusty little port since its founding by the Phoenicians. The upper city, with its narrow streets, tiny pastel houses and whitewashed cave dwellings hugging the looming walls of the **Alcazaba** (*open 10–2 and 4–9*), has retained a fine Moorish feel to this day. Built by Caliph Abd al-Rahman III in the 10th century, the Alcazaba was the most powerful Moorish fortress in Spain; today its great curtain walls and towers defend mostly market- and flower-gardens—nothing remains of the once splendid palace. Behind the fortress, by the wall of Jayrán, you can visit the **Centre for the Rescue of Animals of the Sahara**: before going up, get permission from the centre's headquarters near the tourist office—they'll give you a note letting you wander through the cages and enclosures of a wide variety of endangered animals, in an environment that must feel just like home.

Almería's **cathedral**, begun in 1524, was seemingly built for defence with its four mighty towers. Prettier, and boasting a fine carving of

St James (Santiago) Matamoros and a minaret-like tower, is **Santiago El Viejo**, just off the Puerta Purchena near the top of the Paseo de Almería. It's a bit unusual to find a pilgrimage church, complete with St James's cockle-shells, so far off the main routes.

Almería has a small **archaeological museum** on Calle Javier Sanz, with remains from the remarkable Neolithic culture of Los Millares that flourished here about 3500–3000 BC (*adm free with an EU passport*). You'll learn more about it here than at the sites themselves, but determined Neolithic fans will want to see **Los Millares**, set among stark, barren mountains about 25km north on the N324 at Santa Fe de Mondújar. Five thousand years ago this was rich farmland, and the people who lived here had the leisure to create one of the most advanced prehistoric civilizations in Spain. The burial mounds here are almost true temples, with interior passages and surrounding concentric stone circles, broken by concave semicircular entrances. Five millennia of erosion have made these difficult to make out, and you'll have an even harder time distinguishing the remains of the walled town that once stood nearby.

If you want the **beach**, don't go west. The ocean of plastic under which much of Europe's winter fruit and vegetables ripens, stretched out like a city of the 23rd century between mountains and sea, may have alleviated the hardships of the area but makes for spectacular ugliness too. The beaches only really start to improve west of **Motril**, a dusty town which manufactures chemicals and, like the beaches between it and Almería, is best avoided.

By contrast, east of Almería, the coastal road struggles out to **Cabo de Gata**, with a pretty beach, solitary lighthouse and crystal-clear waters, popular with divers. Inland, the white village of **Níjar** is a charming oasis in an arid setting where potters actively carry on a craft introduced by the Phoenicians. Although the *autovía* has opened Níjar up somewhat to tourism, it's still pretty peaceful outside the summer months and a shopaholic's dream, with it's hand-painted pottery and *jarapa*, distinctive fabrics made, believe it or not, from rags—quite odd en masse but very *World of Interiors* once you get them home. Lorca's play *Blood Wedding* was based on incidents that occurred in Níjar around the turn of the century.

If you're heading to Granada, the north, or up to Murcia, you'll drive through the **Sierra Alhamilla**—one of Spain's driest, most rugged and lunar sierras. The main road east (N340) winds through the northern flanks of the sierra, passing through a lush garden landscape of country estates before rising into a weirdly beautiful but perfectly desolate region, where even in the springtime green is a foreign colour. Here in **Tabernas** are a couple of spaghetti-western sets. At **Mini Hollywood**, the town built by Sergio Leone for such classics as Clint Eastwood's first vehicle, *A Fistful of Dollars*, cowboy shoot-ups and bank robberies are staged at weekends for the benefit of visitors (*open July–Sept; adm*).

Sorbas, with its hanging houses, is most impressively seen from the highway; between the two, the government has decided to exploit the province's greatest natural resource—sunlight—with the country's largest solar energy installation.

Depending upon where your day started, **Mojácar**, 33km on from Sorbas, may be too far for a day excursion. On the other hand, you could do worse than spend a night or two here at Andalucía's northeastern outpost. Isolated amidst the rugged mountains, on a hill 2km from the beach, once-trendy Mojácar has often been compared to a pile of sugar cubes. No town in Spain wears such a Moorish face—its little, flat-roofed, white houses stacked almost on top of one another. Before the equally white hotels were added to the scene a couple of decades ago, the women covered their faces with their veils when passing a stranger; a plaque by the fountain tells how the townspeople valiantly defended themselves against the army of the Catholic Kings. Most unusually, it was the practice of the old women in the village to paint a symbol known as the *indalo* (a stick figure with outstretched arms, holding up an arc) on their doors as a charm against the evil eye and thunderbolts. No one knows when the practice originated, though in the nearby caves of **Vélez-Blanco**, Neolithic drawings of *indalos* dating from 3000 BC have led anthropologists to the conclusion that this is one of the few, if only, cases of a prehistoric symbol being handed down in one place for thousands of years.

Where the Moors went up to the Hills

It had always been thus: all traffic travelling between the city of Granada and the Sierra Nevada inevitably passed this way. First, early Iberian settlers and later, belligerent Moors on horseback, climbing to the peak of Veleta or into Las Alpujarras, must have taken this road. Queen Isabella, Washington Irving and El Caudillo all came trundling round the bend from Granada into Cenes's shanty-town to cross the river and begin the ascent into the Sierra Nevada's silvery landscape. In the mid-1950s, a more regular traffic arose, as students from the University of Granada took the first tentative steps to establishing a permanent ski station in the Sierra Nevada, making winter weekend trips on scooters, in clapped-

Ruta del Veleta

out Fords or any other means of transport which could get them the 30km up to the slopes and back again in time for lectures on Monday morning.

And then came the Ruta del Veleta. Here was a very good *venta* indeed where students, tradesmen and day-trippers could be sure of a good lunch. But it was still a *venta*, no more than a useful little watering-hole on the road to the mountains.

These days, a swish *autovía* encircles Granada and motorists headed for the slopes are deposited via a shiny new slip road on the far side of the river. Nobody passes through Cenes de la Vega any more; by rights, the Pedraza brothers, the owners of Ruta del Veleta, should have cut their losses, shut up shop and gone home. Instead, under their careful management, this humble *venta* has gone from strength to strength; and it's a curious fact that this pit-stop on the wrong side of the tracks is now one of the region's most celebrated restaurants.

Don't take our word for it—try securing a reservation for lunch on a Saturday or Sunday. Unless you're a regular like the Prince of Asturias, you may need all your powers of persuasion.
It would be a shame to come this close to the Alhambra and not make it part of your day, and we propose little more than that. But given the excellence of the cooking at Ruta del Veleta, it may be best to see to that part of your lazy day before you take on lunch.

getting there

From the northeast and the centre of Granada, follow signs to the Sierra Nevada, along the GR420. This road goes straight through Cenes de la Vega, where you'll find Ruta del Veleta at the far end of the village on your right.

From the central car park of the Alhambra (at the top of the hill past the Washington Irving and Guadeloupe hotels), take the road to the right opposite the car park entrance signposted Sierra Nevada. This road joins the GR420 at the bottom of a 1km hill and takes you directly into Cenes de la Vega in five minutes flat. (If you are planning to visit the Alhambra in the morning, this is by far the best way to get to lunch, as it bypasses all of central Granada.)

From Motril and Las Alpujarras, head into Granada on the N323, turning off at Km134 on to the *Ronda Sur* (the A395) and continue as below.

From all other directions (Guadix, Málaga, Antequera and the west) join the *Ronda de Granada* (ring road) going south, following signs for Sierra Nevada and Motril. Turn off at Km134, on to the *Ronda Sur*, signposted to Sierra Nevada and Cenes de la Vega. Now follow signs to Cenes, crossing under the main road, and continuing until the T-junction. Turn left towards the village. Ruta de Veleta is 150m ahead, on the left-hand side.

A word of warning: the new *Ronda Sur* road, the A395, which runs parallel with the GR420, does not appear on Michelin's latest (1996) map.

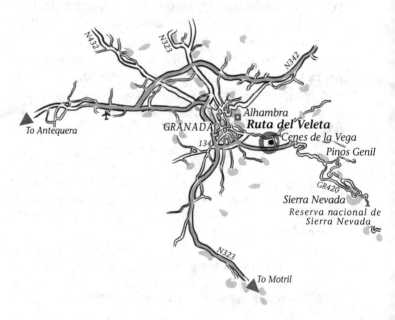

Ruta del Veleta

Carretera de Sierra Nevada 50, Cenes de la Vega (Granada), ℗ (95) 848 61 34. Open daily; booking advisable—essential at weekends. 5500 pts.

Anywhere else it might be kitsch, or at best plain bad taste. At the entrance to the Ruta, a stuffed rabbit complete with spectacles, shooting cap and rifle, stands guard and, surprisingly, he seems rather at home. Alongside him, one of the dynastic Pedraza brothers will greet you, and see that you are ushered—always rather formally—to your table.

The tables are spacious and well-dressed. Down the length of this handsome room, big picture-windows look out to some smallholdings, across the river and upwards to the slopes. Above you, a thousand blue and white, decorative *granadino* wine-jugs uniformly cover the ceiling; while you are admiring them, a white-jacketed waiter will deftly deliver a menu into your hands. Big salads, freshwater fish and game dishes predominate, but the obvious starter is the *tortilla del Sacromonte*. This omelette takes its name from the gipsy area of Granada and used to be made with two or three kinds of offal, such as brains, kidneys and sweetbreads, with the odd testicle thrown in for good measure. The Ruta's version, fried in olive oil and served piping hot from the pan, uses lamb kidneys and ham. Another speciality, *trucha de Riofrío a la mantequilla de anchoas*, trout from Granada's Riofrío river served with anchovy butter, is a robust starter which, like the tortilla, calls for some wine of substance.

The wine list is long and patrician. Two Torres whites stand out, *Waltrau* and *Milmanda*, both complex wines with long finishes. They're also the perfect accompaniment to a main course such as *cazuelita de angulas al ajo verde*, a stew of baby eel with green garlic, one of the Ruta's signature dishes. And the *Milmanda* will support meat dishes too, such as *carre de cabrito al cabor del romero*, roasted kid pungent with rosemary; or *paletilla de cordero asada a la flor del tomillo*, roast shoulder of lamb with thyme.

On the other hand, the big reds are irresistible. *Vega Sicilia*, the star wine of Valladolid, comes in a variety of incarnations dating from 1960, and with prices to match. A middle bracket extravagance, a vintage *Solar de Samaniego* (you'll do no better than the '68) is a wine from Rioja that is lighter in style than most, while an old *Faustino*, from one of Rioja's most respected houses, is no heavier on the palate yet as full and as elegant as a wine can be.

If the service at Ruta del Veleta is a little starchy, it's worth putting up with for the style and pace of the place. The crowd is good-looking and although by any standards the Ruta has now grown rather grand, it still has the buzz of the *venta*. Some may come for an *aperitivo* with a couple of *entremeses*; others will spend the afternoon. In the private dining room, a christening or wedding party may be in full swing and, if it is, you will know about it, for Andalucians are not self-conscious when it comes to celebrating.

Desserts here are more imaginative than one has any right to expect in this land of the freezer. A bowl of wild strawberries from the restaurant's garden—dusted with sugar, soused in *fresa silvestre* liqueur or topped with a great swirl of chantilly cream—is hard to resist. But if there are four of you or more, order *las frivolidades de reposteria Morisca*. It translates rather quaintly as 'Frivolities of the Moorish Confectioner' and, served in this valley between the Alhambra and the Sierra Nevada, on romantic grounds alone is pretty much *de rigueur*.

At this stage, if you are particularly well-dressed or appear sufficiently haughty, one of the Ruta's proprietors will leave his position between the stuffed rabbit and the signed photograph of the Prince of Asturias to come to your table and enquire if all is in order. Ordinary diners are usually left in peace, to muse upon how the disadvantages of a trolley sporting twenty different kinds of *aguardiente* might outweigh the advantages. If you're planning on making the spirally ascent to the ski slopes after lunch, the choice may be decided for you.

Tortilla al Sacromonte

A famous omelette from the Sacromonte area of Granada.

(Serves 4–6)

200g/7oz shelled petit-pois
4 medium-sized potatoes
2 calf or lamb sweetbreads
4 tablespoons olive oil
4 calf or lamb kidneys
8 large eggs, beaten
150g/5oz finely chopped ham
salt and pepper

olive oil

First, cook the petit-pois and set aside. Peel and dice the potatoes into small cubes. Wash and season the sweetbreads, pat dry with kitchen paper and chop fine. In a large omelette pan, heat two tablespoons of the oil over a medium heat. Sauté the kidneys for two to three minutes each side, adding the sweetbreads for 30 seconds or so at the end. Now remove the kidneys and sweetbreads, scraping down the pan, and set all aside on a warm plate. Add the remaining oil to the pan and fry the potatoes over a medium-high heat with the pan covered so they do not crisp. While they are cooking, lightly beat the eggs, and slice the warm kidneys into slivers.

After five minutes, or when the potatoes have softened, add the sweet-breads, kidneys, ham and petit-pois. Combine in the pan, season, then pour in the beaten egg. Cook for three minutes over a medium heat, tipping the pan to let the uncooked egg run to the sides. Next, take a large, warm plate and gently slide the omelette out of the pan and on to the plate—don't turn the omelette out. Now, place the pan upside-down over the omelette and, with your hand placed firmly under the plate, return the omelette swiftly to the pan. Cook for another minute and serve immediately. Tortilla al Sacromonte, *unlike other tortillas, needs to be served piping hot.*

touring around

Granada stands where the foothills of the Sierra Nevada meet the fertile 'Vega de Granada', the greenest and best stretch of farmland in Andalucía. Two of those hills extend into the city itself. One bears the Alhambra, the fortified palace of the Nasrid kings, and the other the Albaicín, the most evocative of the 'Moorish' neighbourhoods of the Andalucían cities. How much you enjoy Granada will depend largely on how successful you are in ignoring the new districts, in particular three barbarically ugly streets that form the main automobile route through Granada: the Gran Vía Colón chopped through the centre of town in the 19th century, the Calle Reyes Católicos and the Acera del Darro. The last two are paved over the course of the Río Darro, the little stream that ran picturesquely through the city until the 1880s.

The Alhambra

The Alhambra and the gardens of the Generalife fall into two distinct parts. You may choose to visit one in the morning, the other in the late afternoon, returning to the **Alhambra** to see it under the stars (*open daily 10–6; also open Tues, Thurs and Sat eve 10–11pm in the summer, 8–10pm mid season; adm 675pts, but all concessions and EU passport holders 300 pts. Admission times constantly change and you are strongly advised to check beforehand with the extremely helpful ticket office, © (95) 822 0912*). The grounds of the Alhambra begin with a bit of the unexpected. Instead of the walls and towers, there is a lovely grove of great elms, the **Alameda**; even more unexpectedly, they are the contribution of the Duke of Wellington, who took time off from chasing the French to plant them during the Peninsular War. Take the path to the left—it's a stiff climb—and in a few minutes you'll arrive at the **Puerta de Justicia**, entrance of the Alhambra. The orange tint of the fortress walls explains the name *al-hamra* (the vermilion), and the unusual style of the carving on the gate is the first clue that here is something very different. The two devices, a hand and a key, carved on the inner and outer arches, are famous. According to one of Washington Irving's tales, the hand will one day reach down and grasp the key; then the Alhambra will fall into ruins, the earth will open, and the hidden treasures of the Moors will be revealed.

From the gate, a path leads up to a broad square. Here are the ticket booth, and the **Puerta del Vino**, so called from a long-ago Spanish custom of doling out free wine from this spot to the inhabitants of the Alhambra. To the left you'll see the walls of the Alcazaba, the fort at the tip of the Alhambra's narrow promontory, and to the right the huge Palacio de Carlos V; signs point your way to the entrance of the Casa Real (Royal Palace), with its splendidly decorated rooms that are the Alhambra's main attraction.

Not much remains of the oldest part of the Alhambra, the **Alcazaba**. This citadel probably dates back to the first of the Nasrid kings. Its walls and towers are still intact, but only the foundations of the buildings that once stood within it have survived. The **Torre de la Vela** at the tip of the promontory has the best views over Granada and the Vega. Its big bell was rung in the old days to signal the daily opening and closing of the water gates of the Vega's irrigation system; the Moors also used the tower as a signal post for sending messages. The Albaicín, visible on the opposite hill, is a revelation: its rows of white, flat-roofed houses on the hillside, punctuated by palm trees and cypresses, provide one of Europe's most exotic urban landscapes.

The highlight of the Alhambra is the **Casa Real** (Royal Palace) (*palace visits are limited to ½hr and the time must be specified at time of ticket purchase, otherwise it will be arranged for approximately 1½hrs later*). Words will not do, nor will exhaustive descriptions help, to communicate the experience of this greatest treasure of al-Andalus. This is what people come to Granada to see, and it is the surest, most accessible window into the refinement and subtlety of the culture of Moorish Spain—a building that can achieve in its handful of rooms what a work like Madrid's Royal Palace cannot even approach with its 2800.

It probably never occurs to most visitors, but one of the most unusual features of this palace is its modesty. What you see is what the Nasrid kings saw, and your imagination need add only a few carpets and tapestries, some well-crafted furniture of wood inlaid with ivory, wooden screens and grilles, and big round braziers of brass for heat or incense, to make the picture complete. Most of the actual building is wood and plaster, cheap and perishable, like a World Fair pavilion; no good Muslim monarch would offend Allah's sense of propriety by pretending that these worldly splendours were anything more than the pleasures of a moment (much of the plaster, wood, and all of the tiles, are the products of careful restorations over the last 100 years). The Alhambra, in fact, is the only substantially intact medieval Muslim palace—anywhere.

Like so many old royal palaces (those of the Hittites, the Byzantines or the Ottoman Turks, for example), this one is divided into three sections: one for everyday business of the palace and government; the next, more secluded, for the state rooms and official entertainments of the kings; and the third, where few outsiders ever reached, for the private apartments of the king and his household.

Of the first, the small **Mexuar**, where the kings would hold their public audiences, survives near the present-day entrance to the palace complex. The adjacent **Patio del Mexuar**, though much restored, is one of the finest rooms of the Alhambra. Nowhere is the meditative serenity of the palace more apparent (unless you arrive when all the tour groups do) and the small fountain in the centre provides an introduction to an important element of the architecture—water. Present everywhere, in pools, fountains and channels, water is as much a part of the design as the wood, tile and stone.

the Alhambra

Where the Moors went up to the Hills

If you have trouble finding your way around, remember the elaborately decorated portals never really lead anywhere; the door you want will always be tucked unobtrusively to the side; here, as in Sevilla's Alcázar, the principle is to heighten the sense of surprise. The entrance to the grand **Patio de los Arrayanes** (Court of the Myrtles), with its long goldfish pond and lovely arcades, is one of these. This was the centre of the second, state section of the palace; directly off it, you pass through the **Sala de la Barca** (Hall of the Boat), so called from its hull-shaped wooden ceiling, and into the **Salón de Embajadores** (Hall of the Ambassadors), where the kings presided over all important state business. The views and the decoration are some of the Alhambra's best, with a cedarwood ceiling and plaster panels (many were originally painted) carved with floral arabesques or Arabic calligraphy. These inscriptions, some Koranic scripture (often the phrase 'Allah alone conquers', the motto of the Nasrids), some eulogies of the kings, and some poetry, recur throughout the palace. The more conspicuous are in a flowing script developed by the Granadan artists; look closely and you will see others, in the angular Kufic script, forming frames for the floral designs.

In some of the chambers off the Patio de los Arrayanes, you can peek out over the domed roofs of the baths below; opposite the Salón de Embajadores is a small entrance (often closed) into the dark, empty **crypt** of the Palacio de Carlos V, with curious echo effects.

Another half-hidden doorway leads you into the third and most spectacular section, the king's residence, built around the **Patio de los Leones** (Court of the Lions). Here the plaster and stucco work is at its most ornate, the columns and arches at their most delicate, with little pretence of any structural purpose; balanced on their slender shafts, the façades of the court seem to hang in the air. As in much of Moorish architecture, the almost overripe arabesques of this patio conceal a subtle symbolism. The 'enclosed garden' that can stand for the attainment of truth, or paradise, or for the cosmos, is a recurring theme in Islamic mystical poetry. Here you may take the 12 endearingly preposterous lions who support the fountain in the centre as the months, or signs of the zodiac, and the four channels that flow out from the fountains as the four corners of the cosmos, the cardinal points, or on a different level, the four rivers of paradise.

The rooms around the patio have exquisite decorations: to the right, from the entrance, the **Sala de los Abencerrajes**, named after the legend of the noble family that Boabdil supposedly had massacred at a banquet here during the civil wars just before the fall of Granada; to the left, the **Sala de las dos Hermanas** (Hall of the Two Sisters). Both of these have extravagant domed *muqarnas* ceilings. The latter chamber is also ornamented with a wooden window grille, another speciality of the Granadan artists; this is the only one surviving in the Alhambra. Adjacent to the Sala de las dos Hermanas is the **Sala de los Ajimeces**, so called for its doubled windows. The **Sala de los Reyes** (Hall of the Kings), opposite the court's entrance, is unique for the paintings on its ceiling, works that would not be out of place in any Christian palace of medieval Europe. The central panel may represent six of Granada's 14th-century kings; those on the side are scenes of a chivalric court. The artist is believed to have been a visiting Spanish Christian painter, possibly from Sevilla.

From the Sala de las dos Hermanas, steps lead down to the **Patio de Lindaraja** (or Mirador de Daraxa), with its fountain and flowers, Washington Irving's favourite spot in the Alhambra. Originally the inner garden of the palace, it was remodeled, along with the surrounding rooms, for the royal visits of Carlos V and Felipe V. Irving actually lived in the **Queen's Chamber**, decorated with frescoes of Carlos V's expedition to Tunis—in 1829 apartments in the Alhambra could be had for the asking! Just off this chamber, at ground-floor level, is the beautifully decorated **hammam**, the palace baths.

Follow the arrows, out of the palace and into the outer gardens, the **Jardines del Partal**, a broad expanse of rose terraces and flowing water. The northern walls of the Alhambra border the gardens, including a number of well-preserved towers: from the west, the **Torre de las Damas**, entered by a small porch, the **Torre del Mihrab**, near which is a small mosque, now a chapel; the **Torre de los Picos**; the **Torre de la Cautiva** (Tower of the Imprisoned Lady), one of the most elaborately decorated; and the **Torre de las Infantas**, one of the last projects in the Alhambra (c. 1400).

Anywhere else, the **Palacio de Carlos V**, an elegant Renaissance building, would be an attraction in itself. Here it seems only pompous and oversized, and our appreciation of it is lessened by the mind-numbing thought of this emperor, with a good half of Europe to build palaces in, having to plop it here—ruining much of the Alhambra in the process. Once Carlos had smashed up the place, he lost interest, and most of the still unfinished palace was not built until 1616.

The original architect, Pedro Machuco, had studied in Italy, and he took the opportunity to introduce into Spain the chilly, Olympian High Renaissance style of Rome. At the entrances are intricately detailed sculptural **reliefs** showing scenes from Carlos's campaigns and military 'triumphs' in the antique manner: armoured torsos on sticks amidst heaps of weapons. This is a very particular sort of art, arrogant and weird, and wherever it appears around the Mediterranean, it will usually be associated with the grisly reign of the man who dreamt of being Emperor of the World. Inside, Machuco added a pristinely classical circular courtyard, based perhaps on a design by Raphael. For all its Doric gravity, the patio was used almost from its completion for bullfights and mock tournaments.

The Palacio de Carlos V contains two **museums**: the **Museo de Bellas Artes** © (95) 822 4843 (*open Tues–Sat 10–2; adm free*); and the **Museo**

Nacional de Arte Hispano-Musulmán ✆ (95) 822 6279 (*open Tues–Sat 9.30–2.30*). On the top floor is the Museo de Bellas Artes, a largely forgettable collection of religious paintings and polychromes from Granada churches. Downstairs, the Museo Nacional de Arte Hispano-Musulmán contains perhaps Spain's best collection of Moorish art, including some paintings, similar to those in the Moorish palace's Sala de los Reyes. Also present are original *azulejo* tiles and plaster arabesques from the palace, and fine wooden panels and screens.

Behind Carlos's palace a street leads into the remnants of the town that once filled much of the space within the Alhambra's walls, now reduced to a small collection of restaurants and souvenir stands. In Moorish times the Alhambra held a large permanent population, and even under the Spaniards it long retained the status of a separate municipality. At one end of the street, the church of **Santa María** (1581), designed by Juan de Herrera, architect of El Escorial, occupies the site of the Alhambra's mosque; at the other, the first Christian building on the Alhambra, the **Convento de San Francisco** (1495), has been converted into a parador.

The Generalife

The Generalife (*opening hours are the same as for the Alhambra; adm included in Alhambra ticket*) was the summer palace of the Nasrid kings, built on the height the Moors called the Mountain of the Sun (*Djinat al-Arif*: high garden). Many of the trillions of visitors the Alhambra receives each year have never heard of it, and pass up a chance to see the finest garden in Spain. To get there, it's about a 5-minute walk from the Alhambra along a lovely avenue of tall cypresses.

The buildings hold few surprises if you've just come from the Alhambra. They are in fact older than most of the Casa Real, probably begun around 1260. The gardens and the view over the Alhambra and Albaicín are transcendent. They are built on terraces, on several levels along the hillside; in the centre, a long pool under a vista of water sprays passes through beds of roses and an infinite variety of other blooms. A lower level, with a promenade on the hill's edge, is broken up into secluded bowers by cypress bushes cut into angular shapes of walls and gateways. There is no evidence that the Moorish gardens looked like this; everything here was done in the last 200 years.

If you're walking down from the Alhambra, you might consider a different route, across the Alameda and down through the picturesque streets below the **Torres Bermejas**, an outwork of the Alhambra's fortifications built on foundations that may be as old as the Romans. The winding lanes and stairways around Calle del Aire and Calle Niño del Rollo, one of the most beautiful quarters of Granada, will eventually lead you back down near the Plaza Nueva.

Albaicín

Even more than the old quarters of Córdoba, this hillside neighbourhood of whitewashed houses and tall cypresses has preserved some of the atmosphere of al-Andalus. Its difficult site and the fact that it was long the district of Granada's poor explain the lack of change, but today the Albaicín looks as if it is becoming fashionable again.

From the Plaza Nueva, a narrow street called the **Carrera del Darro** leads up the valley of the Darro between the Alhambra and Albaicín hills; here the little stream has not been covered over, and you can get an idea of how the centre of Granada looked in the old days. On the Alhambra side, old stone bridges lead up to a few half-forgotten streets hidden among the forested slopes; here you'll see some 17th-century Spanish houses with curious painted *esgrafiado* façades.

Nearby, traces of a horseshoe arch can be seen where a Moorish wall once crossed the river; in the corner of Calle Baruelo there are well-preserved **Moorish baths** (*open Tues–Sat 10–2*). Even more curious is the façade of the **Casa Castril** on the Darro, a flamboyant 16th-century mansion with a portal carved with a phoenix, winged scallop shells and other odd devices that have been interpreted as elements in a complex mystical symbolism. Over the big corner window is an inscription 'Waiting for her from the heavens'. The house's owner, Bernardo de Zafra, was once a secretary to Fernando and Isabel, and seems to have got into trouble with the Inquisition.

Casa Castril has been restored as Granada's **archaeological museum** (*open daily except Mon, 10–2*) with a small collection of artefacts from the huge number of caves in Granada province, many inhabited since Palaeolithic times, and a few Iberian settlements. There is a Moorish room, with some lovely works of art, and finally, an even greater oddity than Casa Castril itself. One room of the museum holds a collection of beautiful alabaster burial urns, made in Egypt, but found in a Phoenician-style necropolis near Almuñécar. Nothing else like them has ever been discovered in Spain, and the Egyptian hieroglyphic inscriptions on them are provocative in the extreme (translations given in Spanish), telling how the deceased travelled here in search of some mysterious primordial deity .

Farther up the Darro, there's a small park with a view up to the Alhambra; after that you'll have to do some climbing, but the higher you go the prettier the Albaicín is, and the better the views. Among the white houses and white walls are some of the oldest Christian churches in Granada. As in Córdoba, they are tidy and extremely plain, built to avoid alienating a recently converted population unused to religious imagery. **San Juan de los Reyes** (1520) on Calle Zafra and **San José** (1525) are the oldest; both retain the plain minarets of the mosques they replaced. Quite a few Moorish houses survive in the Albaicín, and some can be seen on **Calle Horno de Oro**, just off the Darro; on **Calle Daralhorra**, at the top of the Albaicín, are the remains of a Nasrid palace that was largely destroyed to make way for Isabel's **Convento de Santa Isabel la Real** (1501).

Here, running parallel to Cuesta de la Alhacaba, is a long-surviving stretch of Moorish wall. There are probably a few miles of walls left, visible around the hillsides over Granada; the location of the city made a very complex set of fortifications necessary. In this one, about halfway up, you may pass through **Puerta de las Pesas**, with its horseshoe arches. The heart of the Albaicín is here, around the pretty, animated **Plaza Larga**; only a few blocks away the **Mirador de San Nicolás**, in front of the church of that name, offers the most romantic view of the Alhambra with the peaks of the Sierra Nevada behind it. Note the brick, barrel-vaulted fountain on the mirador, a typical Moorish survival; fountains like this can be seen throughout the Albaicín and most are still in use. Granada today has a small but growing Muslim community, and they have cleared the ground just off the mirador to build a mosque. Construction hasn't started yet; apparently they are facing some difficulties with the city government.

On your way back from the Albaicín you might take a different route, down a maze of back streets to the **Puerta de Elvira**; this area is one of the most picturesque corners of the neighbourhood.

For something completely different, you might strike out beyond the Albaicín hill to the **gipsy caves of Sacromonte**. Granada has had a substantial gipsy population for several centuries now. Some have become settled and respectable, others live in trailers on vacant land around town. The most visible are those who prey on the tourists around the Alhambra and the Capilla Real, handing out carnations with a smile and then attempting to extort huge sums out of anyone dumb enough to take one (of course, they'll tell your fortune, too). The biggest part of the gipsy community, however, still lives around Sacromonte in streets of some quite well-appointed cave homes, where they wait to lure you in for a little display of flamenco. For a hundred years or so, the consensus of opinion has been that the music and dancing are usually indifferent, and the gipsies' eventually successful attempts to shake out your last peseta can make it an unpleasantly unforgettable affair. Hotels sell tours for around 2000 pts. Nevertheless, if you care to match wits with the experts, proceed up the Cuesta del Chapiz from the Río Darro, turn right at the **Casa del Chapiz**, a big 16th-century palace that now houses a school of Arab studies, and keep going until some gipsy child drags you home with him. The bad reputation has been keeping tourists away lately so it's now much safer and friendlier as the gypsies are worried about the loss of income. Serious flamenco fans will probably not fare better elsewhere in Granada except during the festivals, though there are some touristy flamenco nightspots—the **Reina Mora** by Mirador San Cristóbal is the best of them. On the third Sunday of each month, you can hear a flamenco mass performed in the San Pedro church on the Carrera del Darro; check for notices at the entrance.

Olive Oil and Firewater in a Country *Comedor*

For 400 years few travellers came this way. The Moorish legacy perhaps too distant, the Renaissance too incidental, this remote corner of Andalucía had long been left to its olive growers. Indeed, the very name Baeza once signified the end of the road for Spaniards.'To go to Baeza' was to go beyond the frontiers of civilization, the back of beyond, a sort of Iberian Timbuktu. The irony of this is that Baeza—along with her elder sister, the ravishingly beautiful Úbeda—are Renaissance jewels which would hold their own with the great architectural centres of northern Spain, or indeed their Italian counterparts in Tuscany and the Veneto. Now, as if to make up for their years of obscurity, both Úbeda and Baeza, a mere 9km apart, are being opened up to tourists at a frantic pace. On a web fanning out from the twin towns, steamrollers lumber along newly-made roads pressing shiny-black tarmac on to barely-dry concrete—part of a production-line churning out new highways with quite indecent haste.

And on the road heading west out of Baeza is a point of quite untypical plainness, where the landscape—as if with the applause of Baeza still ringing in her ears and a few minutes to go before the curtain-up at Úbeda—has been caught backstage with her feet up and no make-up. Here, at this unlikely spot, lies Casa Juanito, a hotel-restaurant whose appearance is best and certainly most kindly described as 'modern' and 'simple' .

The front terrace gives on to the main road—two main roads, in fact—but even if you wanted to sit out here you couldn't, for the brown plastic tables and chairs remain piled high in the corner. Nor do things improve inside as you shuffle, tired and hungry, past a deserted reception area and small bar—similarly deserted and unfashionably decorated with painted mirrors advertising Coca-Cola and Pears Soap, as found in every flea-market from Buenos Aires to Blackpool—in the direction of the dining room. By now, most of you will have turned heel and fled. But not so fast! In Andalucía, you must never judge a book by its cover.

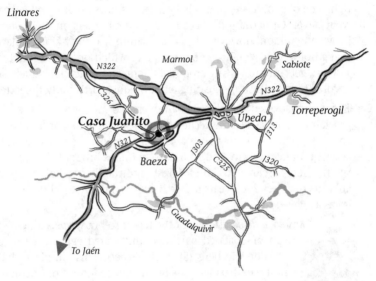

getting there

Baeza lies on the N321, between Jaén and Úbeda. From the north and west travelling on the N1V, bypass the town of Bailén, taking the N322 to Linares. Stay on this road, turning right some 3km beyond Linares, on to the C326 for Baeza.

Travelling from Baeza towards Úbeda, Casa Juanito is on the left-hand side of the road. It stands at an apex corner on the main N321 highway, on the eastern edge of the town next to the Campsa garage, just before the road heads downhill and into open country in the direction of Úbeda.

Casa Juanito

Avenida Puche Pardo 43, 23440 Baeza (Jaén), ✆ (95) 274 0040,
✆ 274 2324. Open Tues to Sat lunch and dinner, and Sun lunch; weekends
and public holidays booking advisable. 5000–6000 pts.

When you find it, chances are that the *comedor* of the Casa Juanito will be full. Dreary, amateurish landscapes hang on the cream-coloured walls. Its serviceable 70s decoration manages to stay just the right side of good taste, precisely because it shows no discernible taste whatsoever. Or perhaps it's because the room borders on the austere. Forget any notion, however, that Casa Juanito is a stuffy kind of place; that's not a word you'd ascribe to a place which opens for lunch at 1.30pm, gets into full swing around 4.00pm, and which is shamelessly devoted to the pleasures of eating and drinking, particularly the latter.

The white-jacketed waiter offers an oversized menu, which proudly proclaims *'la utilización de aceite oliva virgen extra en todos los platos'.* For this is Olive Country with a capital O. Spain is still the world's largest producer of olive oil; the Carthaginians brought the olive to Spain when Tuscany was still a forest, and the Iberians of antiquity knew its qualities 2000 years before it acquired the revered status that it has achieved today.

Ensalada de perdiz, one of the ten or so house specialities, is a salad of poached partridge and grated egg on a bed of shredded iceberg (Spanish: *iseber*). This simple dish is raised to dizzy heights by the final addition of unctuous, unadulterated droplets of *Oro Mágina*, a local Jaén olive oil so fine that it has an acidity level of less than one per cent.

olive oil

Lomo de orza en adobo is a Jaén speciality you will find throughout the province: pressed pork loin, preserved in an earthenware pot, then stunningly brought to life by a generous swirl of *Oro Mágina*. The *faisán con setas*, pheasant with wild mushroms, invokes a Moslem association, with the earthy *setas* (mushrooms) delicately cut out into geometric stars.

The desserts, by contrast, are all latter-day Spanish flamboyance. *Postre de Luisa*—Luisa is the *propietaria*, chef and Juanito's wife—offers a taste of everything that's going, including *cañas borrachas*, impossibly sweet, custard-filled doughnuts; *empanadillas de cabello de angel*, melt-in-the-mouth, fruit-filled *mille-feuilles*; and *gachas*, a milky oatmeal porridge which owes nothing to sophistication but everything to the sweetness of pure sugar.

The wine list at Casa Juanito is excellent—brief almost to the point of curtness but it's quality that counts here, not quantity, with big wines like the vintage Ylleras and a fine Beronia Reserva '85 at small prices.

By half-past four the *comedor* is thick with cigar smoke and environmentally hazardous. In London or New York they'd probably shut the place down, but here in Baeza it's par for the course. The smoke comes at you from all directions: a table of worthies in dark suits wearing expensive watches; a table of unworthies, in shirt-sleeves and wearing even more expensive watches; two local couples out celebrating a modest win on the *lotería primitíva*, injudiciously embarking upon a third bottle of *Yllera '82*.

With coffee comes a complimentary shot of the house *aguardiente*, firewater steeped long and lovingly in anis and cherries. Drink it in one go like the locals and it will knock you off your chair. After that

Casa Juanito

you're on your own. It's not that the waiter will *mind* if you decline to sample more of the 20 or so *aguardientes* on his trolley: he just won't understand how you could forgo such pleasure.

Faisan Relleno estilo Andalusi

The Andalucian hunter loves pheasant, which miraculously seem to proliferate in the sierras of this region for most of the year. The workings of the game calendar are as entrenched as those of the Hacienda *(Spanish Inland Revenue), as* first come, first served *seems to be the general rule.*

If your pheasant is shop-bought and has not been drawn, good signs to look out for are short spurs, which are not very sharp, and a light plumage. This will indicate a young bird. This recipe is sufficient for four with other accompaniments, but is a real treat for two. It's also delicious eaten cold.

(Serves 2–4)

1 pheasant
2 garlic cloves, finely chopped
6 tablespoons olive oil
1 medium onion, chopped
100g/4oz raisins
100g/4oz chestnuts, cooked, peeled and chopped
2 hard-boiled eggs
6 large green olives, chopped
salt and pepper
1 teaspoon caraway seeds
a few coriander leaves, chopped
2 tablespoons pine nuts
2 tablespoons oyster sauce

Preheat the oven to 200°C/400°F (gas mark 6).

Wash and dry the pheasant thoroughly, then rub the skin with the chopped garlic. Heat two tablespoons of the oil in a frying pan and quickly sauté the onion, raisins, chestnuts and olives—no more than three minutes. Season and allow to cool slightly.

Fold the mixture as best you can round the hard-boiled eggs and stuff the bird, securing the opening with a couple of small skewers if necessary. Now drizzle the remaining olive oil all over the bird, sprinkle with the caraway seeds and coriander and place in a roasting tin. Bake in the top part of the preheated oven for 30–40 minutes, depending on the size of the bird.

Meanwhile, scatter the pine nuts over a baking sheet and quickly toast them under a hot grill—don't look away or they'll burn. Also, heat the oyster sauce, or garum, and spread over the base of a warmed serving dish large enough to accommodate the pheasant.

Remove the cooked pheasant from the oven, and keep warm while you make the gravy (see below). Now place the pheasant on the bed of oyster sauce, decorate with the toasted pine nuts and serve with the gravy.

To make the gravy, place the roasting tin over a medium heat, add 150ml/¼ pint of water or stock and stir well to mix it with all the residue in the tin. Bring to the boil and cook for about five minutes. Skim off any grease from the surface of the gravy, season to taste, strain and serve with the pheasant.

touring around

The 13th-century Reconquista was especially brutal to **Baeza**; nearly the entire population fled, many of them moving to Granada, where they settled the Albaicín. The 16th century, by contrast, when the wool trade was booming in this corner of Andalucía, was good to Baeza, leaving it a distinguished little town of neatly clipped trees and tan stone buildings, with a beautiful ensemble of monuments in styles from Romanesque to Renaissance. It seems a happy place, serene and quiet as the olive groves that surround it.

First among the 16th-century monuments is the **cathedral**, on Plaza Santa María. This is a work by Andrés de Vandelvira, an Andalucian architect who created most of neighbouring Úbeda's best buildings. It replaced a 13th-century Gothic church (surviving chancel and portal), which in turn took the place of a mosque; a colonnade from this can be seen in the cloister. For the best show in town, drop a coin in the box marked *custodia* in one of the side chapels; this will reveal, with a noisy dose of mechanical *duende*, a rich and ornate 18th-century silver tabernacle. The fountain in front of the cathedral, the **Fuente de Santa María**, with a little triumphal arch at its centre (1564), is Baeza's landmark and symbol. Behind it is the Isabelline Gothic **Casas Consistoriales**, formerly the town hall.

Heading north on the Cuesta de San Felipe, you pass the 15th-century **Palacio de Jabalquinto**, with an eccentric façade covered with coats of arms and pyramidal stone studs (a Spanish fancy of that age; you can see others like it in Guadalajara and Salamanca). The prettiest corner of the town is a small square, the **Plaza del Pópulo**, enclosed by decorative pointed arches, containing a fountain with four half-effaced lions; the fountain was patched together with the help of pieces taken from the Roman remains at Castulo, and the centrepiece, the fearless lady on the pedestal, is traditionally considered to be Imilce, the wife of Hannibal. In Plaza Cardenal Benavides, the façade of the **Ayuntamiento** (1599) is a classic example of Andalucian plateresque—that heavily ornamented Gothic style of the 16th century—and one of the last.

Even with Baeza for an introduction, **Úbeda** comes as a surprise. It's a near perfect little city. If the 16th century did well by Baeza, it was a golden age here, leaving Úbeda a 'town built for gentlemen', as the Spanish used to say, endowed with one of the finest collections of Renaissance architecture in all of Spain. Two men can take much of the credit: Andrés de Vandelvira and Francisco de los Cobos, imperial secretary to Carlos V, who paid for it all.

Úbeda today leaves no doubt how its local politics are going. In the **Plaza de Andalucía**, joining the old and new districts, there is an old metal statue of a Fascist civil war general named Sero, glaring down from his pedestal. The townspeople have put so many bullets into it, it looks like a Swiss cheese. They've left it here as a joke, and have merrily renamed another square from Plaza del Generalísimo to Plaza 1 de Mayo.

The **Torre de Reloj**, in the Plaza de Andalucía, is a 14th-century defensive tower now adorned with a clock. The plaque near the base, under a painting of the Virgin, records a visit of Carlos V. From here, Calle Real takes you into the heart of the old town. Nearly every corner has at least one lovely palace or church on it. Two of the best can be seen on this street: one is the early 17th-century **Palacio de Condé Guadiana**, with an ornate tower and distinctive windows cut out of the corners of the building, a common conceit in Úbeda's palaces. Two blocks down, the **Palacio Vela de los Cobos** (*open 10–2 and 6–8*) is in the same style, with a loggia on the top storey.

The home of Francisco de los Cobos's nephew, another royal counsellor, was the **Palacio de las Cadenas**, now serving as Úbeda's Ayuntamiento, on a quiet plaza at the end of Calle Real. The side facing the plaza is simple and dignified (the tourist office is here), but the main façade, facing the **Plaza Vázquez de Molina**, is a stately Renaissance creation, the work of Vandelvira.

This is the only place in Andalucía where you can look around and not regret the passing of the Moors, for it is the only truly beautiful thing in all this great region that was not built either by the Moors or under their influence. The Renaissance buildings around the Palacio de las Cadenas make a wonderful ensemble, and the austere landscaping, old cobbles, and a plain six-sided fountain create the same effect of contemplative serendipity as any chamber of the Alhambra. Buildings on the plaza include the church of **Santa María de los Reales Alcázares** (whose restoration is nearly complete), a Renaissance façade on an older building with a fine Gothic cloister around the back; the parador, a magnificent 16th-century palace whose open courtyard is the perfect spot for an early evening drink; two sedate Renaissance palaces; and Vandelvira's **Sacra Capilla del Salvador**, begun in 1540, the finest of Úbeda's churches and where Cobos is buried.

Behind El Salvador, the **Hospital de los Honrados** has a delightful open patio—but only because the other half of the building was never completed. South of the plaza, the end of town is only a few blocks away, encompassed by a street called the **Redonda de Miradores**, a quiet spot favoured by children and goats, with remnants of Úbeda's wall and exceptional views over the Sierra de Cazorla to the east.

Indeed, it is the **views** which truly move the spirit in this part of Andalucía. In all of Spain, there is no more concentrated an area of olive groves than here in northeastern Jaén. They stretch as far as the

eye can see, uninterrupted in every direction, and continue to the far reaches of the province and beyond. The panoramic vistas from the main roads are impressive enough, but if you have the feeling that you would like to get *into* the landscape, try a short but spectacular drive around Úbeda. Coming from Baeza on the N321, turn right onto the newly-built C325 just before the town of Úbeda begins. After 8km, turn left on to the J320, little more than a dirt track, forking left after 5km on to the J313 which, after a further 15km, brings you to the small town of **Torreperogil**. This is a drive more thrilling than any roller coaster or theme-park simulator, and the austerely beautiful landscape takes on a unforgettable physical and sensual presence.

Torreperogil is a humdrum place, but gives its name to a particularly good local table wine, *El Torreño*. The co-operative headquarters, in **Calle España**, sells this wine—as well as *Oro Mágina* olive oil at almost embarrassingly low prices.

And so, with your car boot crammed with oil and *El Torreño* the day winds slowly down and you must decide in which direction to turn. Back west, perhaps, to a base at Úbeda or Jaén; or south towards Granada; or onwards to the eastern sierras, and the enchanted wonderland of the Cazorla National Park?

The Little Chef, Baena-style

Southeast of Córdoba, within the triangle bordered by Granada, Antequera and Córdoba itself, lies the Parque Natural de la Sierra Subbética. An area of 'outstanding natural beauty' this may have been designated, but the olive-rich Subbética's beauty is only skin-deep. It's a harsh region, where the deceptive softness of the land lies in inverse proportion to the toil of cultivating it.

Here the oil-presses are eyesores and huge metal storage tanks blot out the landscape.

The N432, looping uneconomically between Córdoba and Granada, once sported *ventas* by the score; you can see them still, unloved, unwanted roadside ruins. The young have upped and gone and those who remain, *campesinos* (farmers) by day, prefer in the evening and at weekends to go into the town to play *hidalgo* (the

Huerta de San Rafael

gentleman). The roadside *venta* in this corner of Andalucía has had its day.

Then, a couple of bends past the cheerful market town of Baena—as the road straightens out after a series of turns and the rather aggressively industrial-agricultural landscape begins to relax and recede—a grinning cardboard cut-out on your right invites you to stop. He's the Little Chef of the Subbética— and while he's not a sophisticated chap, he runs the best kitchen for miles around. Next stop for good food is Granada, 100km away. Drive on at your peril.

getting there

The Huerta de San Rafael lies on the main Granada–Badajoz (Córdoba) highway, between Baena and Luque.

Travelling southeast from Córdoba, continue through Baena. A couple of kilometres after the town, just after the turning to the confusingly-named Marbella, the restaurant is on your right. Travelling north from Granada, the restaurant will appear on the left-hand side of the road, just past the first turn-off sign for Luque.

Huerta de San Rafael

Carretera Badajoz–Granada Km340, Baena (Córdoba), © (95) 766 7497.
Open daily. About 2500 pts.

About the only thing proprietor Francisco Ortiz Valera doesn't do when you pull up at Huerta San Rafael is put out the red carpet. Otherwise, the welcome is five-star, whether you're a teenage couple on a Vespa in from the farm for a *copita* and a *tapa,* or a middle-aged couple from Haywards Heath 'doing' southern Spain in an air conditioned Audi, looking for a blow-out in this gastronomically-challenged corner of Andalucía.

The front-room of this *venta* is a bar, where marble-topped tables and a state-of-the-art counter feel more provincial French than rural Spanish. But the Huerta's like an onion, layer upon layer of different rooms. Carry on through the bar and discover another, a mini-dining room with some fine old conquistador chests; then another, all pottery and lace curtains; yet another beyond, unheated and empty with antlers and a skeleton; and still one more, Francisco's own sitting room with TV going full-blast and a couple of tables laid-up ready for a lunch-time rush.

Kick-off with a glass of Montilla, Cordoba's sherry with its big, grapey flavour, and consider the menu. *Surtido de canapés*, which owes more perhaps to smorgasbord than *cocina Andalús*, is a tangy assortment of salmon, fresh anchovy and elver, and makes a good summer starter, while *mojama,* salt-cured tuna, is a delicacy rare to find out in the country. Hot starters include some excellent *revueltos*, individual ramekins of scrambed egg with prawn, string-beans, spinach and cured ham, or, best of all in the spring, wild asparagus.

Main courses are a showcase for the region's specialities. A *churrasco,* a succulent fillet of white pork seared to perfection on a white-hot grill and served with a pungent *aioli*, is big enough for four. The *cochifrito ibérico,* fried piglet, will titillate the palate—ears, cheeks and trotters included. *Truchas con jamón*, a surf-and-turf dish of trout stuffed with ham, is actually based upon a recipe from Navarra, but takes advantage of

Baena olive oil and Trevélez mountain ham. And speaking of ham, the *flamenquines caseras*, homemade croquettes of ham rolled with cheese and fried in deep, hot oil are a taste sensation. Order them as a main dish or to share as a *tapa*.

 Since fish and white meat are so predominant on this menu, it's a good idea to stick with white wine. The wine list is small, but an interesting choice might be Montilla-Moriles' *Vino Verde*, a young 'green' wine whose Portuguese cousin may be more familiar. The *Cordobésa* variety, still a very young wine, is fruitier and less innocuous.

Dessert, as so often in Andalucía, means a selection from the freezer, though a velvety *flan de piñones*—crème caramel with pine nuts—has a subtle and *casero* (homemade) flavour to it. Washed down with delicate cups of extraordinarily strong espresso, it's a fitting end to a very elegant lunch.

Afterwards, you can walk it off with a stroll round Francisco's garden; there's even a swimming pool for the benefit of *bona fide* travellers.

Truchas con Jamón

This is a dish from Navarra which Francisco Ortiz has adapted to take full advantage of the produce of the South: river trout, mountain ham and extra virgin olive oil.

(Serves 4)

4 medium trout
8 thin slices of Serrano ham
flour
6 tablespoons olive oil
juice of 4 lemons
knob of butter
parsley or dill, to garnish
salt and pepper

Slit the trout along the belly, clean, and remove the backbone by spreading the fish out and pressing the flesh-side of the fish against a board—but leave the head and tail intact. Now wash the fish and pat dry with kitchen paper. Place two thin slices of ham in the cavity of each fish. Now dredge each fish lightly with the flour, shaking off the excess.

In a frying pan large enough to hold the four fish without crowding, heat the oil until hot, but not smoking. Now sauté the fish for about five minutes on each side, until nicely browned. Remove the fish to a warm plate, then scrape down the pan and, off the heat, add all the lemon juice and knob of butter. Return to the heat and, as the sauce starts to bubble, return the fish to the pan, warming quickly on both sides.

Serve at once, pouring lemon sauce over each fillet and seasoning and garnishing with parsley or dill, as desired.

---

touring around

The Sierra Subbética is a large and relatively featureless area, but there are pockets of interest. None more so than the ancient town of **Baena** and its surrounding area.

Situated 60km southeast of Córdoba, Baena was an Iberian settlement before the arrival of the Romans. Under the Roman occupation it flourished, becoming an important social and cultural centre and, eventually, provincial capital. Little survives from this time—just the foundations of a bridge over the Guadalquivir, a ruined temple and the Lion of Baena, excavated in 1923 and now in the Archaeological Museum in Madrid.

It was in Roman times, however, that the town's pre-eminence as 'olive-oil capital' of Andalucía dates. Baena still produces arguably the finest olive oil in Spain, with strict methods of production and a resulting zero per cent acidity. You can visit **Nuñez de Prado** olive mill, Calle Cervantes 15, ✆ (95) 767 0141 (*9.30–1.30 and 4–7, or by appointment, except Oct and Nov*), to see a working mill and oil production plant in operation.

olive oil

In the centre of town, the arcaded **Almacén**, off the handsome Plaza de la Constitución, is an 18th-century warehouse now used as a cultural centre. On the Calle Henares, the 16th-century Gothic church of

Santa María, gutted by fire during the Civil War, still boasts a beautiful altar-screen, for which the church is justly famous. A little further brings you to **La Madre de Dios,** a 16th-century *mudéjar* (Moorish-influenced) convent, partly open to the public, where you can buy produce made by the nuns, including honey and sweet cakes. Baena's main annual event is its Holy Week celebrations, when an ear-splitting drum-rolling competition is held to see who can play longest and loudest.

Two nearby villages, **Luque** and **Zuheros**, make good excursions from the town. **Luque,** 7km southeast of Baena, is a 13th-century village teetering on the clifftops with splendid ruins of a Moorish castle which you can wander around. **Zuheros,** 5km west of Luque on the CO241 in a loop from Baena, is a magnificent Subbética hill-village, nestling in a gorge with peaks behind. The **Iglesia de los Remedios** incorporates a tower built from a minaret: the village fell to Fernando III in 1240 and became a frontier post against the kingdom of Granada.

Behind the village, the **Cueva de Murcielagos,** or Cave of Bats (it shares a name with a grotto in Granada province), has stalactites, stalagmites and prehistoric cave paintings—though the last are in poor condition and you'll need a guide to locate them.

About 4km further round the loop brings you to **Doña Mencia,** an unprepossessing oil-producing town with a ruined 15th-century castle and a small viniculture museum. From Doña, a 14km drive south on the C327 brings you to **Cabra,** a delightful town with a charming old quarter as well as a number of Baroque *palacios*. The church of **San Juan Bautista,** known locally as **San Juan de Cerro,** is reckoned to be one of Spain's oldest, dating back to the 7th century. The **Iglesia de la Asuncíon,** a Baroque church built over a mosque, boasts a fine interior with twisted marble columns; its gardens of palms and cypresses are an oasis of tranquillity for strolling on a spring or summer evening. It's a good spot too to bid farewell to the region: look out across a sweeping landscape towards the Sierra Nevada to the southeast or the Guadalquivir valley to the north—and decide which way to turn.

White Heat

Like an Arab *souk*, the streets around Córdoba's great Mezquita cathedral teem with traders. The yellow and sepia Kodak signs above the dingy kiosks may be 40 years old, but the film they sell is brand new, for the coach-trade is booming here and business is brisk in this touristic corner of southern Spain.

On the doorsteps of the uninviting restaurants, with their back-breaking Spanish chairs and unappetizing *menús del día*, waiters in slightly grubby white shirts and black bow-ties stand smoking *Ducados*, urging you to step inside. Eating in Córdoba is fraught with hazard.

There is an alternative. In the Calle Romero, in the heart of the Judería, lies El Churrasco. No undiscovered jewel this: El Churrasco has been around for 25 years. Nor is it grand: handsome certainly, and historic—it occupies the

El Churrasco

14th-century house of a Jewish nobleman—but the design is abysmal with waiters frequently queuing to pass through an undersized archway, and the window of the ladies' loo opening out on to the main dining room.

What makes El Churrasco so special is its atmosphere. It is urbane, it is sophisticated in the best sense, and it is *totally* Spanish. The service is brusque, sometimes to the point of discourtesy. Perhaps this is what puts tourists off for, despite being lauded in guide books and recommended by every hotel concierge in the city, you'd be hard pressed to find a non-Spaniard in the place.

It has been said that restaurants should be an extension of their environments. It's this principle that makes La Coupole, Harry's Bar and Simpsons-in-the-Strand so agreeable. It is also what makes El Churrasco the most exciting restaurant in Andalucía, and one you will want to return to again and again.

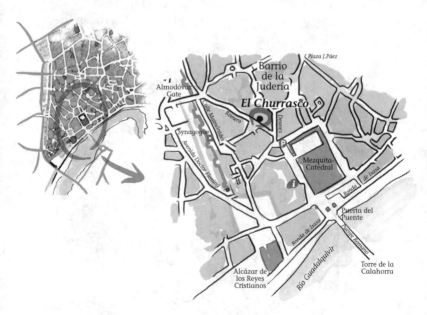

getting there

El Churrasco is located in the Barrio de la Judería, the old Jewish quarter of Córdoba. If you come to Córdoba by car, park in one of the public car parks off the Paseo de la Victoria, and make your way on foot to the great cathedral of Córdoba, universally known as La Mezquita, or Mosque, in deference to its original status.

Leaving the square of the Mezquita by the northwest corner, via Calle Herreros, turn right after a few yards into Manriquez Deanes, then almost immediately left into Romero. You will find El Churrasco 100m along Romero, on the right-hand side.

El Churrasco

Romero 16 (Judería), 1403 Córdoba, ✆ (95) 729 0819, ✇ (95) 729 4081. Open daily except Aug, 1pm–4pm and 8.30–midnight. Booking essential: request the courtyard. 5000 pts.

The anteroom to the main restaurant is a crowded bar through which you will have to fight your way, before announcing your arrival to a waiter who will probably ignore you. Behind the counter, the white-hot *churrascos* are going full pelt, with slabs of meat lining up to be seared and grilled.

Eventually you will be shown to a table: the nicest place to sit is the courtyard: heated in winter, air-conditioned and protected by a thick awning from a fierce sun in summer. Every good Spaniard hopes to pass this way at least once in a lifetime. As you walk to your table, all eyes will be upon you. Every detail of your demeanour, your clothes and your bearing will be scrutinized and immediate disinterest will then be feigned. Order a glass of Montilla, Córdoba's own variety of *vino de Jerez*, and they'll know immediately you're an out-of-towner who's read the guide book. Try playing the Córdobeses at their own game instead: order a whisky-Coke or a *Cuba Libre*. You won't fool them completely, but you'll certainly confuse them.

El Churrasco is such a landmark, it has evolved a cuisine of its own. *Salmorejo*, once the food of the poor, is a generic term for a cold, tomato-based soup, which is a second cousin of the more familiar *gazpacho*. It is the classic dish at El Churrasco: subtle, smooth and thick. A plate of *berenjenas fritas*, pastilles of fried aubergine dribbled with olive oil, can be left in the middle of the table for all to try.

But it's meat that really counts here. *Churrasco* is the name not only for the white hot grill, it's also the term for a fillet of pork, long, lean and cooked in an instant over the coals. There is also a large selection of cuts of red meat, including *solomillo de bola* (a Châteaubriand the size of a brick), *chuletón de buey del valle de los Pedroches* (the T-bone of this famous local beef is big enough for four); and *pierna de cordero al horno* (roast leg of lamb). *Solomillo de ternera* is a sirloin of white veal cooked on the *churrasco.*

You'll have the leisure to pursue the pastime so beloved of fellow diners at the restaurant: observing their fellow diners. At a corner table, a couple in late middle-age keep up a continuous public display of affection. You know they must be married—to each other—for the courtyard of El Churrasco is no place for a private tryst. A young bull-fighter—barely 17-years-old with a fine Roman nose and sideboards shaved to razor-sharp points—sits between two spivvy promoters. They ply him with *chinchón dulce*, and soon he will sign whatever they propose. At the next table, a fiery redhead throws back her flame-coloured hair and catches the eye of every man in the room. Her companion is bald and she is a good three inches taller, but his patience is great and his wallet fat. She orders a plate of *profiteroles* and teasingly offers him one—sweeter and smoother than she.

Puddings here definitely play up to the Spanish sweet tooth, though there are some exceptions: the chocolate mousse is bitter and rich and tends to run out early—reserve it when you order your first courses—and the lemon sorbet with Champagne is packed with flavour.

 El Churrasco has one of the finest cellars in Spain. It is now so extensive, it has moved into another building along the street, impeccably maintained and restocked by owner Rafael Carrillo. The house wines, a rich, round Valdepeñas *tinto* and an oaky, local Montilla white, cost less less than 500 pts for a demi-carafe. Try them both before moving on to something

memorable: a Gran Reserva Rioja, for example, at less than half the price you would pay in Madrid.

So, now the bullfighter has signed his contract and the promoters, deal clinched, are anxious to leave. The redhead is bored. The lovers in the corner have wasted the siesta hour holding hands and giggling over a second bottle of *Benjamín*, and now he will be late back at the office. The waiters roll back the awning: the sun has long since dipped behind the Mezquita. And now you too must tear yourself away.

Salmorejo

The classic soup of Córdoba appears at first sight to be a gazpacho, but it's thicker, creamier and arguably less refined than the traditional cold tomato soup of the south. It requires no cooking, the thickening process being achieved by a method of slowly adding oil, not dissimilar to making mayonnaise. Despite being decorated with boiled eggs and dainty cubes of ham, Salmorejo is still considered in some quarters to be a dish of the poor.

(Serves 4)

8 large fresh tomatoes or 2 x 400g/14oz tins peeled plum tomatoes
3 garlic cloves, chopped
2 tablespoons wine- or cider-vinegar
8 slices stale white bread, crusts removed and crumbed
150ml/5fl oz olive oil
salt and pepper
4 small eggs, hard-boiled and quartered
150g/5oz good ham or pancetta, cubed
2 tablespoons chopped fresh parsley

If you are using fresh tomatoes, soak them for a couple of minutes in boiling water, then remove the skins. Roughly chop the tomatoes and put them into a food processor together with the garlic, vinegar and bread crumbs. Now switch on and, after a few seconds, with the motor still running, pour in the olive oil in a slow, steady stream.

Remove the mixture from the food processor and leave to stand for a couple of hours in the fridge. The soup will thicken further as the bread swells. Remove the soup from the fridge 15 minutes before serving and add cold

*water as necessary to achieve the desired consistency. Add salt and pepper
to taste and decorate with the quarters of hard-boiled egg, cubes of ham
and chopped parsley.*

touring around

Lunching in the heart of **Córdoba**, it makes sense to spend the rest of
the day exploring this fascinating city. It's definitely worth stopping
at the regional tourist office at Calle Torrijos 10, ✆ (95) 747 12 35, to
get a detailed map, for Córdoba has the biggest and most labyrinthine
old quarter in Spain. To arrange personal guides to the cathedral
and other sights, call ✆ (95) 748 6997 or 741 0629, or turn up at the
cathedral itself.

La Mezquita

La Mezquita (*open Mon–Sat 10–7, Sun 1.30–7 in summer; daily 10.30–
5.30 in winter; adm 750 pts, free before 10am and Sun*) is the local name
for Abd ar-Rahman's Great Mosque. It means 'mosque' and even
though the building has officially been a cathedral for 750 years, no
one could ever mistake its origins. In AD 756 Abd ar-Rahman, founder
of a new state, felt it necessary to construct a great religious monument for his capital. As part of his plan, he also wished to make it a
centre of pilgrimage to increase the sense of divorce from eastern
Islam; Mecca was at the time held by his Abbasid enemies. Islam was
never entirely immune to the exaltation of holy relics, and there is a
story that Abd ar-Rahman had an arm of Mohammed to legitimize his
mosque as a pilgrimage site. The site, at the city centre, had originally
held a Roman temple of Janus, and later a Visigothic church.

Only about one-third of the mosque belongs to the original.
Successive enlargements were made by Abd ar-Rahman II, al-Hakam
and al-Mansur. Expansion was easy: the plan of the mosque is a
simple rectangle divided into aisles by rows of columns, and its size
was increased to serve a growing population simply by adding more
aisles. The result was the second largest of all mosques, exceeded only
by the one in Mecca. After 1236 it was converted for use as a cathedral
without any major changes. In the 1520s, however, the city's clerics
succeeded in convincing the Royal Council, over the opposition of

the Córdoba city government, to allow the construction of a choir and high altar, enclosed structures typical in Spanish cathedrals. Carlos V, who had also opposed the project, strongly reproached them for the desecration when he saw the finished work—though he himself had done even worse to the Alhambra and Sevilla's Alcázar.

Most people end a visit to La Mezquita somewhat confused. The endless rows of columns and red-and-white striped arches make a picture familiar to most of us, but actually to see them in this gloomy old hall does not increase one's understanding of the work. They make a pretty pattern, but what does it mean? It's worth going into some detail, for learning to see La Mezquita the way its builders did is the best key we have to understanding the refined world of al-Andalus.

Before entering, take a few minutes to circumnavigate this massive, somewhat forbidding, pile of bricks. Spaced around its 685m of wall are the original entrances and windows, excellent examples of Moorish art. Those on the western side are the best, from the time of al-Mansur: interlaced Visigothic horseshoe arches, floral decorations in the Roman tradition, and Islamic calligraphy and patterns, a lesson in the varied sources of this art.

The only entrance to the mosque today is the **Puerta del Perdón**, a fine *mudéjar* gateway added in 1377, opening to the **Patio de los Naranjos**, the original mosque courtyard, planted with orange trees, where the old Moorish fountain can still be seen. Built into the wall of the courtyard, over the gate, the original minaret—a legendary tower said to be the model for all the others in al-Andalus—has been replaced by an ill-proportioned 16th-century bell tower. From the courtyard, the mosque is entered through a little door, the **Puerta de las Palmas**, where they'll sell you a ticket and tell you to take off your hat. Inside, it's as chilly as Sevilla Cathedral.

Now here is the first surprise. The building is gloomy only because the Spanish clerics wanted it that way. Originally there was no wall separating the mosque from the courtyard, and that side of the mosque was entirely open. In the courtyard, trees were planted to continue the rows of columns, translating inside to outside in a remarkable tour-de-force that has rarely been equalled in architecture. To add to the effect, the entrances along the other three walls would have been open to the surrounding busy markets and streets. It isn't just a trick of architecture, but a way of relating a holy building to the life of the city around it. In the Middle East there are many medieval mosques built on the same plan; the pattern originated with the first Arabian mosques, and later in the Umayyad Mosque of Damascus, one of the first great shrines of Islam. In Turkey they call them 'forest' mosques, and the townspeople use them like indoor parks, places to sit and reflect or talk over everyday affairs. In medieval Christian cathedrals, whose doors were always open, it was much the same. The sacred and the secular become blurred, or rather the latter is elevated to a higher plane. In Córdoba, this principle is perfected.

In the aesthetics of this mosque, too, there is more than meets the eye. Many European writers have seen it as devoid of spirituality, a plain prayer-hall with pretty arches. To the Christian mind it is difficult to comprehend. Christian churches are modelled after the Roman basilica, a government hall, a seat of authority with a long central aisle designed to humble the suppliant as he approaches the praetor's throne (altar). Mosques are designed with great care to free the mind from such behaviour patterns. In this one, the guiding principle is a rarefied abstraction—the same kind of abstraction that governs Islamic geometric decoration. The repetition of columns is like a meditation in stone, a mirror of Creation where unity and harmony radiate from innumerable centres.

Another contrast with Christian churches can be found in an obscure matter—the distribution of weight. The Gothic masters of the Middle Ages learned to pile stone upwards from great piers and buttresses to amazing heights. Córdoba's architects amplified the height of their mosque only modestly by a daring invention—adding a second tier of arches on top of the first. They had to, constrained as they were by the short columns they were recycling from Roman buildings, but the result was to make an 'upside-down' building, where weight increases the higher it goes, a play of balance and equilibrium that adds much to the mosque's effect.

There are about 580 of these columns, mostly from Roman ruins and Visigothic churches the Muslims pulled down; legend credits La Mezquita with a thousand originally. Some came from as far as Constantinople, a present from the emperors. The same variety can be seen in the capitals—Roman, Visigothic, Moorish and a few mysteries. The surviving jewel of the mosque is its **mihrab**, added in the 10th century under al-Hakim II, an octagonal chamber set into the wall and covered by a beautiful dome of interlocking arches. A Byzantine emperor, Nikephoras Phokas, sent artists to help with its mosaic decoration, and a few tons of enamel chips and coloured glass cubes for them to work with. That these two states should have had such warm relations isn't that surprising; in those days, any enemy of the Pope and the western Christian states was a friend of Constantinople. Though the *mihrab* is no longer at the centre of La Mezquita, it was at the time of al-Hakim II; the aisle extending from it was the axis of the original mosque.

Looking back from the *mihrab*, you will see what once was the exterior wall, built in Abd ar-Rahman II's extension, from the year 848. Its gates, protected indoors, are as good as those on the west façade, and better preserved. Near the *mihrab* is the **Capilla de Villaviciosa**, a Christian addition of 1377 with fancy convoluted *mudéjar* arches that almost succeed in upstaging the Moorish work. Behind it is a small chapel usually closed off. Fortunately, you can see most of the **Capilla Real** above the barriers; its exuberant stucco and *azulejo* decoration are among the greatest works of *mudéjar* art. Built in the 14th century as a funeral chapel for Fernando IV and Alfonso XI of Castile, it is contemporary with the Alhambra and shows some influence of the styles developing in Granada. Far more serious intrusions are the 16th-century Coro (choir) and Capilla Mayor (high altar). Not unlovely in themselves, they would not offend anywhere else but here. Fortunately, La Mezquita is so large that from many parts of it you won't even notice them. Begun in 1523, the plateresque Coro was substantially altered in the 18th century, with additional stucco decoration, as well as a set of Baroque choir stalls, by Pedro Duque Cornejo. Between the Coro and Capilla Mayor is the tomb of Leopold of Austria, Bishop of Córdoba at the time the works were completed (and, interestingly, Charles V's uncle). For the rest of the Christian contribution, dozens of locked, mouldering chapels line the outer walls of the mosque. Never comfortable as a Christian building, today the cathedral seems to be hardly used at all, and regular Sunday masses are generally relegated to a small corner of the building.

Around La Mezquita

Below La Mezquita, along the Guadalquivir, the melancholic plaza called **Puerta del Puente** marks the site of Córdoba's southern gate with a decorative **arch** from 1571, celebrating the reign of Felipe II. The very curious 'churrigueresque' (florid Baroque) monument next to it is called the **Triunfo** (1651) with a statue of San Rafael (the angel Raphael). Wild Baroque confections such as this are common in Naples and south Italy (under Spanish rule at the time); there they are called *guglie*. Behind the plaza, standing across from La Mezquita, is the **Archbishop's Palace**, built on the site of the original Alcázar, the palace of Abd ar-Rahman.

The **Roman bridge** over the Guadalquivir probably isn't Roman at all any more; it has been patched and repaired so often that practically nothing remains of the Roman work. Another statue of Raphael can be seen in the middle—probably replacing an old Roman image of Jupiter or Mercury. The stern-looking **Calahorra Tower** (1369), built over Moorish foundations, once guarded the southern approaches of the bridge; in its time it has been a prison and a girls' school, but now it contains a small **museum** (*open daily 10.30–6*) of Córdoba's history, with old views and plans of the city, and the armour of Gonzalo Fernández de Córdoba, the 'Gran Capitán' who won much of Italy for Fernando and Isabel. It also has an historical multivision extravaganza, which is expensive and probably only of interest to the dedicated tourist.

Just to the west, along the river, Córdoba's **Alcázar de los Reyes Cristianos** was rebuilt in the 14th century and used for 300 years by the officers of the Inquisition. There's little to see, but a good view of La Mezquita and the town from the belvedere atop the walls. The **gardens** (*open daily 9.30–7*) are peaceful and lovely, an Andalucían amenity much like those in Sevilla's Alcázar. On the river's edge you'll see an ancient **waterwheel**. At least some of the Moors' talent for putting water to good use was retained for a while after the Reconquista—until Queen Isabel came to stay at the Alcázar and found her dreams disturbed by the sounds of the mill; after a few nights she ordered it to be dismantled, and it was rebuilt only in the early 1900s. If you continue walking along the Guadalquivir, after about a kilometre you'll come to Parque Cruz Conde and the new **Córdoba zoo** (*open daily 10am to sunset*), where you can see a rare black lion, who probably doesn't enjoy being called 'Chico'.

The Judería

As in Sevilla, Córdoba's ancient Jewish quarter has recently become a fashionable area, a nest of tiny streets between La Mezquita and Avenida Dr Fleming. Part of the Moorish walls can be seen along this street, and the northern entrance of the Judería is the old **Almodóvar gate**. The streets are tricky, but the Calle Maimónides and the 14th-century synagogue are well signposted. The **synagogue** (*open daily except Mon, 10–2 and 3.30–5.30; adm free for EU citizens*) stands behind a high wall, adjacent to a flowering garden. Inside, the Hebrew inscriptions and Alhambra-style arabesques are all well preserved; the upstairs ladies' gallery remains intact and the recess for the ark, facing eastwards towards Jerusalem, is clearly visible.

On Plaza Maimónides is the **Museo Taurino** (*open daily 9.30–1 and 5–7.30 in summer, 5.30–8.30 in winter*), which is devoted mainly to bullfighting. Manolete and El Cordobés are the city's two recent contributions to bullfighting culture; here you can see a replica of Manolete's sarcophagus, the furniture from his home and the hide of Islero, the bull that did him in, along with more bullfight memorabilia than you ever thought existed. The turn-of-the-century Art-Nouveau posters are beautiful, and among the old prints you can pay homage to the memory of the famous taurine malcontent Moñudo, who ignored the *toreros* and went up into the stands after the audience.

White Neighbourhoods

From the mosque you can walk eastwards through well over a mile of twisting white alleys, a place where the best map in the world wouldn't keep you from getting lost and staying lost. Though it all looks much the same, it's never monotonous. Every little square, fountain or church stands out boldly, and forces you to look at it in a different way than you would a modern city—another lesson in the Moorish aesthetic.

The streets themselves have probably changed little since 1236, but their best buildings are a series of **Gothic churches** built soon after the Reconquista. Though small and plain, most are exquisite in a quiet way. Few have any of the usual Gothic sculptural work on their façades, to avoid offending a people accustomed to Islam's prohibition of images. The lack of decoration somehow adds to their charm. There are a score of these around Córdoba, and nothing like them elsewhere in the south of Spain. **San Lorenzo**, on Calle María Auxiliadora, is perhaps the best, with a rose window designed in a common Moorish motif of interlocking circles. Some 15th-century frescoes survive around the altar and on the apse. **San Pablo** (1241), on the street of the same name, is early Gothic (five years after the Christian conquest) but contains a fine *mudéjar* dome and ceiling. **San Andrés** on Calle Varela, two streets east of San Pablo, **Santa Marina** on Calle Morales, and the **Cristo de los Faroles** on Calle Alfaros are some of the others. Have a look inside any you find open; most have some Moorish decoration in their interiors, and many of their towers (like San Lorenzo's) were originally minarets. **San Pedro**, off Calle Alfonso XII, was the Christian cathedral under Moorish rule, though largely rebuilt in the 1500s.

The neighbourhoods have other surprises, if you have the persistence to find them. **Santa Victoria** is a huge austere Baroque church on Calle Juan Valera, modelled after the Roman Pantheon. Nearby on Plaza Jerónimo Páez, a fine 16th-century palace houses the **National Archaeological Museum** (*open Tues–Sun 9–2.30; adm, but free for EU citizens*), the largest in Andalucía, with Roman mosaics, a two-faced idol of Janus that probably came from the temple under La Mezquita, and an unusual icon of the Persian *torero*-god Mithras; also some Moorish-looking early Christian art, and early funeral steles with odd hieroglyphs. The large collection of Moorish art includes some of the best work from the age of the caliphate, including finds from Medinat az-Zahra.

A *Campo de Tiro* on the Dusty Road to Carmona

The remains of Sevilla's Expo '92 now lie crumbling, and the air of decay which has settled upon the Isla de la Cartuja Expo site bodes ill for its partial re-opening, promised for 1996. But Expo brought with it many long-term benefits, none more prized than a new era of communications linking Andalucía's

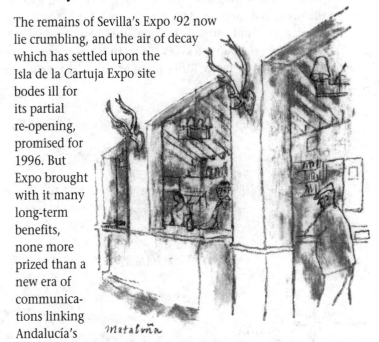

Matalvña

capital, Spain's fourth largest city, with the rest of the country.

Sevilla's new airport, San Pablo, is the envy of European airport directors—unique in that it runs well below capacity; a new railway line slashes the journey time for the 530km between Sevilla and Madrid to a mere two hours. And then there are the roads: inner orbitals, outer orbitals, and brand new highways to Huelva, Cádiz, Córdoba and beyond.

But the six-lane monster which snakes eastwards out of the city towards Carmona can still, under a burning Andalucian sun, seem long and dusty. It becomes dustier still as you turn off the main *carretera* some 10km out of the city on to a dirt track that takes you, past pines and hedgerows, towards the *Campo de Tiro*, the Mataluña firing range.

At Mataluña you can shoot clay birds or, if you prefer, join one of the organized shoots and go after the real thing. You'll find quail, pheasant and partridge in abundance here, once you have mastered the idiosyncrasies of the Andalucian game season—it often seems as if they make up the rules on a day-to-day basis.

Another option is to shoot nothing at all, but repair instead to the low-slung lodge where owner Fernando Oriol will welcome

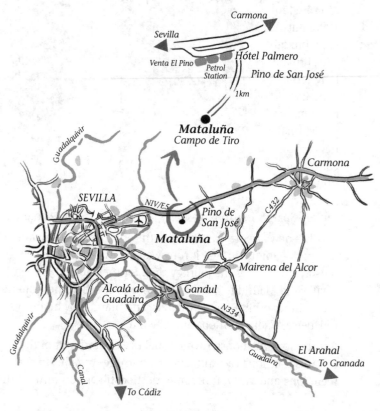

A Campo de Tiro on the Dusty Road to Carmona

you to his ranch-style restaurant with its pleasing intimacy, un-fancy menu and hearty country cooking.

getting there

On the N1V travelling east between Sevilla and Carmona, turn right at the Km524 road sign. Coming from the opposite direction, cross over the highway via the bridge at Km525, turning off the *carretera* at Km524 (travelling east) as above. Now drive along the service road that runs alongside the *carretera*. Passing the Venta El Pino and next to it a petrol station, you turn right at the Hotel Palmero, following the track for about 1km and keeping left where the road forks. A dip in the track and a short incline brings you to the perimeter fence of the Mataluña estate. Drive through the gate to park in front of the lodge.

Mataluña

Pino de San José (Sevilla), © (95) 468 7007. Open Tues–Sun throughout the year; book weekends. About 2000 pts.

At first glance you could be forgiven for thinking you had just walked into the beer garden of an English country pub. There are some unsightly plastic slides for children to play on, rough wooden benches are nailed immovably to the ground, and there's no sign of anyone to take your order. Just as you're beginning to work yourself up into a thoroughly disgruntled frame of mind, Fernando, or one of his seemingly numberless assistants, appears from behind the heavy, hessian blinds that keep the interior cool and dark in summer. He is armed with a dish of plump, purple olives, slivers of ham, and Mataluña's simple *carta*. At this point, things start to look up.

There are separate menus here for summer and winter. The summer dishes are lighter, as you would expect, with the emphasis on cold soups, salads, and a well-prepared *pechuga de pollo*, chicken breast in a delicate sauce of cream and tarragon. In the winter months, you can sample a wide variety of game, as well as Mataluña's speciality, *cabrillas*. These local snails are particularly meaty and the helping here is generous to say the least: about 15 per person, served sizzling in an earthenware casserole. As you prise them from the shell using tooth-pick, fork or fingers, you may catch the unmistakable beat of a *sevillana* coming from an ancient wireless in the vicinity of the kitchen and, once again, the mood of Andalucía steals upon you.

Fernando brings forth the next courses: *faisan*, a young pheasant poached in stock and served on a mound of buttery rice; or an *entrecôte de ternera*, a juicy, griddle-lined steak, that Spanish hybrid which is neither as bland as veal nor as strong as matured beef. It is served with two sauces, both of which you dollop generously on to your plate: a tangy, cumin-spiked, homemade mustard, and pungent *alioli* mayonnaise.

Time perhaps to order another bottle of *Lebrija*, a modest, local table wine which you might quite rightly regard with suspicion else-where; but here, in the province of Sevilla, it tastes surprisingly fine. It makes a good foil too to the sweetness of *natillas*, Mataluña's rich, homemade egg-custard, smooth and sweet on the tongue.

An occasional burst of gunshot way in the distance breaks the stillness of the afternoon. You down your soot-black coffee and sip your wine; in the lazy afternoon sun the bottle quickly grows warm, but is no less delicious for that. You thought you might try your hand at some clay-pigeon shooting after lunch; you thought you might, but by now it's half-past five; the shadows are beginning to lengthen; the sound of others shooting is strangely satisfying. You catch the watchful eye of Fernando standing in the doorway, and motion to him to bring you another bottle.

Cabrillas a la Mataluña

Caracoles *are snails; they are eaten throughout Spain, enjoyed in a variety of ways: steamed, casseroled, in a* paella *with fish or in a stew with rabbit. The local snail, the* cabrilla, *is found in abundance in this part of Andalucía, and is a year-round favourite. Unlike their French cousins, here snails are eaten as a hearty main course.*

(Serves 4)

48 medium-sized snails
salt
300ml/½ pint white vinegar
4 tablespoons olive oil
2 large onions, finely chopped
8 garlic cloves, peeled
450g/1lb tin peeled plum tomatoes
scant half bottle white wine

The preparation of snails is not for the squeamish. In order to purge them, they need to be fasted for a couple of days then boiled for about five minutes. If time is of the essence, they can be boiled in a deep pan for 45 minutes, turning the heat up vigorously for the last few minutes (this will cause the snails to froth). Remove the snails from their shells, then wash them several times in a mixture of the vinegar and salt water. If following the method below, carefully dry them in a teatowel.

Heat the oil in a large, flameproof casserole; add the onions and garlic, and when the onions begin to soften, add the tomatoes, roughly chopped. After ten minutes, when you have a good, thick paste, add the snails and, when they are bubbling nicely, turn the heat up high and add the wine. Cook for a few minutes until the wine has reduced, then lower the heat to a gentle simmer for a further 45 minutes.

Serve piping hot with good, doughy bread for mopping up the juices.

---

touring around

Mataluña is less than half an hour by car from downtown Sevilla, so you can spend a full morning sightseeing before driving out here for lunch. Travelling east from Sevilla on the N1V, you cross **La Campina**, a vast tract of flatland between the **River Guadalquivir** and the **Cordillera hills**. Some 20km further brings you to **Carmona**, a sizeable town and a Sevilla in miniature where there is a great deal to see and do.

Actually, it's probably much older than Sevilla. Remains of a Neolithic settlement have been found around town; the Phoenician colony that replaced it grew into a city and prospered throughout Roman and

Moorish times. Pedro the Cruel favoured it and rebuilt most of its extensive Alcázar. Sitting proudly on top of the town, with views over the valley, this fortress is now a national parador.

Carmona is well worth exploration. Its walls, mostly Moorish fortifications built over Roman foundations, are still standing, including a grand gateway on the road to Sevilla, the **Alcázar de la Puerta de Sevilla** (*open Fri and Sat 11–1*). Continue through the arch and up to the palm-decked Plaza de San Fernando, where the under-16s and over-60s gather; the Ayuntamiento here has a Roman mosaic of Medusa in its courtyard. Next, take Calle Martín López up to the lofty 15th-century church of **Santa María** (*open daily except Mon 10–12, 7–8 and Sun 11–12, 7–8*), built on the site of an old mosque . The old quarters of town have an ensemble of fine palaces, and *mudéjar* and Renaissance churches. On one of these, **San Pedro** (1466), you'll see another imitation of La Giralda of Sevilla, La Giraldilla. Though not as fussily ornate as her big sister, she has a cleaner exterior. Carmona's prime attraction, however, is the **Roman necropolis** (*open daily except Mon, 10–2 and 4–6, Sun 10–2*), a series of rock-cut tombs off Avenida Jorge Bonsor. Some, like the 'Tomb of Servilia', are elaborate creations with subterranean chambers and vestibules, pillars, domed ceilings and carved reliefs . Near the entrance to the site are remains of the Roman amphitheatre, forlorn and unexcavated.

If you're based in Sevilla and heading back there the same day, you might prefer to make a circular tour of the area which will eventually bring you back to the city. Ask at Mataluña for directions to **Mairena del Alcor**, then follow the C432 for 7km to **Alcalá de Guadaira**, a fascinating small town. Standing on the river of the same name, it was originally settled in the copper age, nearly 5000 years ago. More recently, it became a Moslem stronghold named Al-Kalat Wadaira, and the town has changed little in the intervening centuries. The large Almohad castle, with 11 towers, is well preserved and impressive.

Just 3km east of Alcalá lies **Gandul**, with some of its Arabic walls still standing and the impressive, megalithic tomb of **Los Alcores**. From here, it's a short way back to Sevilla on the N334. And as darkness falls on a sultry summer evening, you may well find that this is the dustiest road of them all.

'Dios te de salud y gozo, y casa con corral y pozo'

Corral del Agua

'Persepolis in August was cool compared to this,' said our well-travelled, name-dropping friend as we snaked through Sevilla's Barrio de Santa Cruz at lunchtime looking for the Corral del Agua. It was still early in June but the thermometer read 40°C in the shade.

This magnificent city has a climate as extreme as its history: summers of blistering heat when the well-off *sevillanos* shut up shop and leave town and the less well-off live behind drawn shutters; winters when rain-clouds wrap around the city like a shroud for a week at a time and old women curse and have chill-blains. And benign seasons too, clement days when the sun rises early and sets late, but never climbs too high nor grows too hot—days when the scent of orange blossom hovers over the city like an enchanted mist, permeating every corner with its drowsy magic.

But today was not such a day. As we crossed the Plaza de Doña Elvira, the temperature seemed to rise yet higher. Our friend did not look as if he'd make it across the square. 'One more corner and we're there,' we told him and so we were, standing exhausted in front of the handsome gates of the Corral.

A swift and knowing waiter showed us to our table in the corner of the courtyard, cool, green and naturally shaded. He brought refreshing glasses of *tinto de verano* and a bottle of mineral water so cold that steam rose from it. Our friend looked around. 'Hmm,' he observed in spite of himself, looking at the marble fountain and wishing-well (for his breed do not usually hold with cutesy wishing-wells), 'this is very charming.'

Indeed it is: in fact, when the thermometer goes way up, for our money Corral de Agua is the most charming restaurant in the whole of the province.

getting there

Corral de Agua has an enchanting location next to Washington Irving's house in the Barrio de Santa Cruz, Sevilla's old Jewish quarter. It is accessible only on foot.

From the Plaza del Triunfo, the square between the cathedral and the entrance to the Alcázar, enter the Barrio via the exquisitely proportioned Patio de Banderas. In the top left-hand corner follow the alleyway called Judería. This opens out onto Vida. Keeping to the right, the square becomes Callejón del Agua. The Corral is located just after the first corner on your left.

From the train station and the north of the city, enter the Barrio via the Jardines de Murillo at the Plaza de Santa Cruz, another of the Barrio's beautiful squares. The next square to the south is Plaza de Alfaro, which in turn leads to Callejón del Agua, in the south-west corner. Coming from this direction, you will find the Corral on your right, just after Justino de Neve.

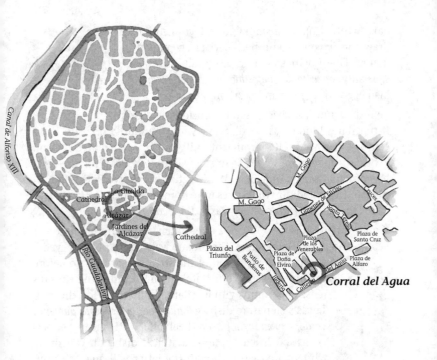

Corral del Agua

Callejón del Agua 6, 41004 Sevilla, ℗ (95) 422 0714. Open daily except Sun, 1–4 and 8–12; closed Jan. Booking essential for outside tables. About 4000 pts.

If you eat in the beautiful garden of the Corral, the chances are you'll never venture inside. The 17th-century house is better proportioned than most in the Barrio and, although the downstairs rooms are cavernous, there's an air of elegance here—punctuated by starched pink and white linen and gleaming silver cutlery. With its easy manners born of impeccable pedigree, the Corral is equally at home with *Sevillanos* and visitors. It's that elusive quality again—a restaurant which welcomes tourists but is not a tourist restaurant.

Chef Angel Lucas specializes in modern Andalucian cooking. *Pochas con almejas* is a fragrant dish of steamed clams and white beans; an oaky white Rioja or a smoky, dry, local Lebrija to draw the flavour would be a perfect accompaniment. These wines would also suit another speciality, *revuelto de langostinos y cebolletas*, scrambled egg with prawns and pearl onions.

Refreshed and revitalized, stop to consider the Corral. It translates literally as 'yard'. Some yard: the fountain is late 18th-century, the well dates from antiquity and the ancient trees and exotic shrubbery are set off against a wall of '*ladrillo*' pink, the rose-hue of Renaissance Andalucía. Washington Irving lived next door in the late 1820s and the two houses were immortalized as *La Hostería del Laurel* in Zorilla's 19th-century classic *Don Juan Tenorio*.

If your intention is to 'do' Sevilla after lunch, order another bottle of Lebrija and put ice cubes in it. The urbane waiter won't bat an eyelid. If you plan to skulk round the streets of the Barrio before heading back to your hotel room, dip into the Corral's reds: a plummy vintage Barbadillo might fit the bill. Lucas's signature dish, *solomillo de ternera a la pimienta verde, con manzana frita*, beef fillet with green peppercorns and fried apple, is a stylish dish you can drink white or red with, though the latter will give the beef, from Asturias' wet pasturelands, its proper due.

Corral del Agua has enough self-esteem not to mind whether you eat one course or four. But with an afternoon sun raging and the city deep in siesta, you'd be mad to give up the benison of a shady table one minute sooner than necessary. A *mousse de chocolate*, prosaic in name but epic in stature, is the perfect excuse to prolong your stay, washed down with *café solo* and a glass of *licor de manzana*.

Other tourists come and go; an American matron ties the strings of her oversized sun-hat and gathers her brood; the well-fed *sevillano* lawyer across the courtyard dips his napkin in a glass of mineral water and dabs a spot on his Loewe tie, then starts a leisurely stroll back to his air-conditioned office; a pert little *chica* who will be late back at the family store slaps the cheek of her companion, a man from the motor trade, and tells him that her mother was right all along.

'Dios te de salud y gozo, y casa con corral y pozo'

('God give you health and joy, and a house with
a yard and a well')

runs the inscription in this enchanted garden. And at this moment,
suspended in time and space in a courtyard in Andalucía, who are you
to wish for more?

Pochas con Almejas

A wonderfully versatile dish of white beans and clams, pochas con
almejas *can be enjoyed as a warming winter hot-pot or, eaten cold, as part
of an elegant summer buffet. It also makes an excellent* tapa, *which you
can of course enjoy at any time of year.*

(Serves 4)

*200g/7oz dried white kidney beans or 650g/1 ½lbs tinned beans,
    such as haricot or cannellini*

1 onion, peeled and quartered

1 garlic clove

1 bouquet garni

salt and pepper

1kg/2 ¼lbs clams

scant ¼ bottle white wine

2 tablespoons extra virgin olive oil

*If using dried beans, soak them in a large pan of unsalted water overnight.
(If you use tinned beans, they will not be as firm to the bite as dried cooked
beans.) When you are ready to start cooking, drain off the soaking water
and fill the pan with fresh cold water until you have enough to cover them
by about three fingers. Add the onion, clove of garlic, bouquet garni and
pepper. Cover the pot, bring to the boil and simmer for about an hour.*

*While the beans are cooking, thoroughly wash the clams, and put them
into a large saucepan. Barely cover them with water, pour in the white wine
and bring to the boil. Cook until they open—shaking the pan will
encourage them. As soon as they have cooled enough to handle, remove
the clams from the shells, reserving the cooking liquid.*

Strain the beans. Add the clams and the reserved cooking liquid and continue to cook for a further five minutes. The beans should still have 'bite', but they should not be mushy. Allow to cool a minute or two, then add salt and pepper to taste and drizzle the olive oil over before serving.

---

touring around

Sevilla, like the great Italian cities, needs time, patience and, most of all, stamina. Between the months of May and September, when temperatures soar, stamina is something invariably in short supply.

The best advice is 'take it easy'. You can't hope to see it all, not even in a week; but a leisurely day or two, spent largely out of doors with an undemanding schedule, may prove the most worthwhile way to see the city. Start the morning by climbing the Giralda: it will acclimatize you to the city and give you your bearings. The Archive of the Indies is open mornings only, so if erudition is your thing, head over to the Avenida de la Constitución or stroll round the monumental cathedral and pay homage to Christopher Columbus before going into the Barrio for lunch.

After lunch, when the shadows at last begin to lengthen, is the perfect time to amble round the Barrio, and the luxuriant gardens of the Alcázar.

La Giralda

A good place to start your tour of Sevilla is at one of Andalucía's most famous monuments, La Giralda, (*open Mon–Sat 11–5; Sun and hols 10.30–1.30; adm 300 pts, or 600 pts including entrance to the cathedral*). You can catch its 97m tower peeking over the rooftops from almost anywhere in Sevilla; it will be your best friend when you get lost in the city's labyrinthine streets. This great minaret, with its *ajimeces* and brickwork arabesques, was also built under the Almohads, from 1172 to 1195, just 50 years before the Christian conquest. The surprisingly harmonious spire stuck on top is a Christian addition. Whatever sort of turret originally stood on top was surmounted by four golden balls (or apples, according to one chronicler) stacked up at the very top, designed to catch the sun and be visible to a traveller one day's ride from the city; all came down in a 13th-century earthquake. On the top of their spire, the Christians added a huge, revolving statue of Faith as a weathervane (many writers have noted the curious fancy of having a supposedly constant Faith turning with the four winds). La Giralda, the weathervane, has given its name to the tower as a whole.

The climb to the top is easy; instead of stairs, there are shallow ramps—wide enough for Fernando III to have ridden his horse up for the view after the conquest in 1248.

The Cathedral

For a while after the Reconquista, the Castilians who repopulated Sevilla were content to use the great Almohad mosque, built at the same time as La Giralda. At the turn of the 1400s, in a fit of pious excess, it was decided to build a new cathedral (*open Mon–Sat 11–5; Sun and holidays 2–4*) so grand that 'future ages shall call us mad for attempting it'. If they were mad, at least they were good organizers— they got it up in slightly over a century. The architects are unknown, though there has been speculation that the original master was either French or German.

The exterior, with its great rose window and double buttresses, is as fine as any of the Gothic cathedrals of northern Spain—if we could only see it. Especially on the west front, facing the Avenida de la Constitución, the buildings close in; walking around its vast bulk, past the fence of Roman columns joined by thick chains, is like passing under a steep, ragged cliff. Before it was cleaned to look pretty for the World Fair the grime contributed to the effect. Some of the best original sculptural work is on the two portals flanking the main door: the **Puerta del Bautismo** (left), and the **Puerta del Nacimiento** (right).

The groundplan of this monster, roughly 120m by 180m, probably covers the same area as did the mosque. On the northern side, the **Patio de los Naranjos** (Patio of the Orange Trees, and planted accordingly) preserves the outline of the mosque courtyard. The Muslim fountain (built around a basin from the previous Visigothic cathedral) survives, along with some of the walls and arches. In the left-hand corner, the Moorish 'Gate of the Lizard' has hanging from it a stuffed crocodile, said to have been a present from an Egyptian emir asking for the hand of a Spanish *infanta*. Along the eastern wall is the entrance of the **Biblioteca Colombina**, an archive of the explorer's life and letters.

The cavernous interior (*open Mon–Sat 11–5; Sun and holidays 2–4*) overpowers the faithful with its size more than its grace or beauty. The main altarpiece is the world's biggest *retablo*, almost 37m high and entirely covered with carved figures and golden Gothic ornament; it took 82 years to make, and takes about a minute to look at. The cathedral is dark and cold inside, and without the usual nave and transept; the enormous space is ill-defined and disorienting. Just behind the Capilla Mayor and the main altar, the **Capilla Real** contains the tombs of San Fernando, conqueror of Sevilla, and of Alfonso the Wise; Pedro the Cruel and his mistress, María de Padilla, are relegated to the crypt underneath. The art of the various chapels around the cathedral is lost in the gloom, but there are paintings by Murillo in the Capilla de San Antonio (in the north aisle), and an altarpiece by Zurbarán in the Capilla de San Pedro (to the left of the Capilla Real).

In the southern aisle, four stern pall-bearers on a high pedestal support the tomb of **Christopher Columbus.** They represent the kingdoms of Castile, León, Navarre, and Aragón. Columbus has been something of a refugee since his death. In the 16th century his remains were moved for unknown reasons from Valladolid to the island of Santo Domingo, and after Dominican independence from there to Havana cathedral. In 1899, after Cuba became independent, he was brought to Sevilla, and this idiosyncratic monument, put up to honour him. In the Dominican Republic, they'll tell you Columbus is still buried in Santo Domingo. Of course, most Spaniards are convinced Columbus was born in Spain, so it is appropriate that the life of this most elusive character should have mysteries at both ends.

Most of the cathedral's collections are housed in a few chambers near the turnstiles at the main entrance. In the **Sala Capitular**, which has an *Immaculate Conception* by Murillo, Sevilla's bishop can sit on his throne and pontificate under the unusual acoustics of an elliptical Baroque ceiling. The adjacent **sacristy** contains paintings by Zurbarán, Murillo, Van Dyck and others, most in dire need of restoration. Spare a moment for the reliquaries. Juan de Arfe, maker of the world's biggest silver monstrances, is represented here with one that seems almost a small palace, complete with marble columns. Spain's most famous, and possibly most bizarre reliquary, is the **Alfonsine Tables**, filled with over 200 tiny bits of tooth and bone. They were said to have belonged to Alfonso the Wise and were made to provide extra-powerful juju for him to carry into battle.

In common with most of its contemporaries, parts of Sevilla's cathedral were public ground, and the porches, the Patio de los Naranjos, and often even the naves and chapels were used to transact all sorts of business. A 16th-century bishop put an end to this practice, but prevailed upon Felipe II to construct next to the cathedral an exchange, or **Lonja**, for the merchants. Felipe sent his favourite architect, Juan de Herrera, then still busy with El Escorial, to design it. The severe, elegant façades are typically Herreran, and the stone balls and pyramids on top are practically the architect's signature. By the 1780s little commerce was still going on in Sevilla, and what was left of the American trade passed through Cádiz, so Carlos III converted the lonely old building to hold the **Archive of the Indies** (*open weekdays, 10–1; research, by appointment, 8–3; © (95) 421 1234*), the repository of all the reports, maps, drawings and documents the crown collected during the age of exploration. The collection, the richest in the world, has not even yet been entirely sifted through by scholars; but it is always worth a look.

The Alcázar

It's easy to be fooled into thinking the Alcázar (*open Tues–Sat 11–5, Sun and holidays 10–1; June–Sept, Tues–Sat, 10–1.30 and 5–7; closed Mon; adm 700 pts*) is simply a Moorish palace; some of its rooms and courtyards seem to come straight from the Alhambra. Most of them, however, were built—by Moorish workmen—for King Pedro the Cruel of Castile in the 1360s. The Alcázar and its king represent a fascinating cul-de-sac in Spanish history and culture, and allow the possibility that al-Andalus might have assimilated its conquerors rather than have been destroyed by them.

Pedro was an interesting character. In Froissart's *Chronicle*, we have him described as 'full of marveylous opinyons... rude and rebell agaynst the commandementes of holy churche'. Certainly he didn't mind having his Moorish artists, lent by the kings of Granada, adorn his palace with sayings from the *Koran* in Kufic calligraphy. Pedro preferred Sevilla, still half-Moorish and more than half-decadent, to Old Castile, and he filled his court here with Moorish poets, dancers and bodyguards—the only ones he trusted. But he was not the man for the job of cultural synthesis. The evidence, in so far as it is reliable, suggests he richly deserved his honorific 'the Cruel'; although to *Sevillanos* he was Pedro the Just. His brother Don Fadrique is only one of many he is said to have assassinated in this palace. One of the biggest rubies among the British crown jewels was a gift from Pedro to the Black Prince—he murdered an ambassador from Granada to get it off his turban.

Long before Pedro, the Alcázar was the palace of the Moorish governors. Work on the Moorish features began in 712 after the capture of Sevilla. In the 9th century it was transformed into a palace for Abd ar-Rahman II. Important additions were made under the Almohads; the Alcázar was their capital in al-Andalus. Almost all the decorative work you see now was done under Pedro, some by the Granadans and the rest by Muslim artists from Toledo; altogether it is the outstanding production of *mudéjar* art in Spain.

The Alcázar is entered through a little gate on the Plaza del Triunfo, on the south side of the cathedral. The first courtyard, the **Patio de la Montería**, has beautiful arabesques, with lions amid castles for Castile and León; this was the public court of the palace, where visitors were received, corresponding to the Mexuar at the Alhambra. At the far end of the Patio is the lovely **façade** of the interior palace, decorated with inscriptions in Gothic and Arabic scripts.

Much of the best *mudéjar* work can be seen in the adjacent halls and courts; their seemingly haphazard arrangement was in fact a principle of the art, to increase the surprise and delight in passing from one to the next. The **Patio de Yeso** (Court of Plaster) is largely a survival of the Almoravid palace of the 1170s, itself built on the site of a Roman *praetorium*. The **Patio de las Doncellas** (Court of the Maidens), entered through the gate of the palace façade, is the largest of the courtyards, a little more ornate than the rooms of the Alhambra—built at the same time and possibly by some of the same craftsmen.

The Patio de las Doncellas leads to the **Salón de los Embajadores** (Hall of the Ambassadors), a small domed chamber that is the finest in the Alcázar despite jarring additions from the time of Charles V. In Moorish times this was the throne room. Another small court, the **Patio de las Muñecas** (Court of the Dolls) where King Pedro's bodyguards cut down Don Fadrique, takes its name from two tiny faces on medallions at the base of one of the horseshoe arches—a little joke on the part of the Muslim stone-carvers. The columns here come from the ruins of Medinat az-Zahra.

Spanish kings after Pedro couldn't leave the Alcázar alone. Fernando and Isabel spoiled a large corner of it for their **Casa de Contratación**, a planning centre for the colonization of the Indies. There's little to see in it: a big conference table, Isabel's bedroom, a model of the *Santa María* in wood and a model of the royal family (Isabel's) in silver. Charles V added a **palace** of his own, as he did in the Alhambra. This contains a spectacular set of **Flemish tapestries** showing finely detailed scenes of Charles's campaigns in Tunisia.

Within its walls, the Alcázar has extensive and lovely **gardens**, with reflecting pools, palm trees, avenues of clipped hedges, and lemons and oranges. The park is large, but you can't get lost unless you find the little **labyrinth** near the pavilion built for Charles V in the lower gardens. Outside the walls, there are more gardens, a formal promenade called the **Plaza Catalina de Ribera**, with two monuments to Columbus, and the **Jardines de Murillo**, small though beautifully landscaped, bordering the northern wall of the Alcázar.

East of the Cathedral

If Spain envies Sevilla, Sevilla envies **Barrio Santa Cruz**, a tiny, exceptionally lovely quarter of narrow streets and whitewashed houses. It is the true homeland of everything *sevillano,* with flower-bedecked patios and iron-bound windows through which the occasional nostalgic young man still manages to get up the nerve to embarrass his sweetheart with a serenade.

Before 1492 this was the Jewish quarter of Sevilla; today it's the most aristocratic corner of town. In the old days there was a wall around the Barrio; today you may enter through the Jardines de Murillo, the

Calle Mateos Gago behind the cathedral apse, or from the **Patio de las Banderas**, a pretty Plaza Mayor-style square next to the Alcázar. On the eastern edge of the Barrio, **Santa María la Blanca** (on the street of the same name) was a pre-Reconquista church; some ancient details remain, but the whole was rebuilt in the 1660s, with spectacular rococo ornamentation inside and paintings by Murillo.

On the eastern fringes of the old town, the Barrio Santa Cruz fades gently into other peaceful pretty areas—less ritzy, though their old streets contain more palaces. One of these, built by the Dukes of Medinaceli (1480–1571) is the **Casa de Pilatos** (*open daily 9–6; adm 1000 pts, concessions 500 pts*) on Plaza Pilatos. The dukes like to tell people that it is a replica of 'Pontius Pilate's house' in Jerusalem. (Pilate, without whom Holy Week would not be possible, is a popular figure; there's a common belief that he was a Spaniard.) It is a pleasant jumble of *mudéjar* and Renaissance work, with a lovely patio and lots of *azulejos* everywhere.

The entrance, a mock-Roman triumphal arch done in Carrara marble by sculptors from Genoa, leads through a small court into the **Patio Principal**, with 13th-century Granadan decoration, beautiful coloured tiles, and rows of Roman statues and portrait busts—an introduction to the dukes' excellent collections of antique sculpture in the surrounding rooms, including a Roman copy of a Greek herm (boundary marker, with the head of the god Hermes), imperial portraits, and a bust of Hadrian's boyfriend, Antinous.

Behind the Casa de Pilatos, **San Esteban**, rebuilt from a former mosque, has an altarpiece by Zurbarán; around the corner on Calle Luis Montoto are remains of an Almoravid **aqueduct**. A few streets away to the northeast, the **Palacio de la Condesa de Lebrija**, is worth a visit for its fine Roman mosaics brought from Itálica. On Calle Águilas, **San Ildefonso** has a pretty yellow and white 18th-century façade. Another post-1492 palace with *mudéjar* decoration, several streets north on Calle Bustos Tavera, is the huge **Palacio de las Dueñas**.

The Knifeman Cometh

casa del Corregidor

Despite the Junta de Andalucía's marketing initiative which aims to create a *Ruta de los Pueblos Blancos*, a sort of Disney-trail Route of the White Villages, one fact is incontrovertible: these *pueblos* are idyllic. And if the great cities of al-Andalus are the virtuosos, it's the trill, peal and chimes of the white villages which complete the magnus opus of present-day Andalucía.

Arcos, strewn along a ridge high above the Guadalete valley, fits the bill perfectly. 'A poor-man's Ronda,' you may read in your guide book, and certainly it looks like Ronda in miniature. 'Impregnable fortress', you will see in another—and, yes, Alfonso the Wise must surely have had a hard time of it when he took the town from the Moors in 1264. 'Typical white village', a third will tell you—but here you must draw the line. There's no such thing as a typical white village and, if there were, Arcos would not be it.

In his book *Sierras of the South*, Alastair Boyd remembers his first visit here in the late 1950s. He and his wife were followed by a strange-looking individual who pressed his services upon them as a guide. At the far end of town, he was behind them still, and when they entered a bar to get rid of him, he followed them in and sat down at their table. The barman, seeing what was going on, came over to the table to persuade their persecutor to leave them alone. At this, the man drew a knife and slashed the barman across the arm. The police were called and statements taken. Later that night, the man was out and about on the streets again. According to Boyd he became a parking attendant in the Plaza de España, with all the authority vested in him by a uniform and cap.

Anita Richmond, an eccentric hispanophile with an unhealthy interest in the occult, had plied Boyd with tales of madness and interbreeding in Arcos and claimed that covens were still active in the old town at the time of his visit.

All this, of course, adds greatly to its mystery and its appeal. The 16th-century magistrate's house, Casa del Corregidor, rebuilt in the 1960s in its original style, stands on the main square at right angles to the church of Santa María, and now serves as the town's parador. After what you've heard of Arcos, you may find it reassuring to eat in the house of the local lawman.

getting there

From the eastern Costa del Sol via Ronda, take the C339 in the direction of Algondales, continuing on the N342 to Arcos (61km).

From the western Costa del Sol, the C440 (13km west of San Roque) through Los Barrios; turn right on to the C343 for Arcos at the Medina Sidonia crossroads.

Starting from Cádiz and the Costa de la Luz, follow the A4 Sevilla *autopista*, taking the Arcos exit N342 just east of Jerez. From Jerez the N342 takes you directly to Arcos.

Follow signs to *Centro Cuidad* and *Parador*, negotiating an extremely narrow main street which will eventually bring you to the Plaza de Cabildo (Plaza de España). The Parador (Casa del Corregidor) is on the left-hand side of the square as you enter.

Casa del Corregidor

Plaza de Cabildo s/n, Arcos de la Frontera 11630 (Cádiz), ✆ (95) 670 0500, ✆(95) 670 1116. Open daily 1–4pm and 8–10.30pm. About 4000 pts. (Menú Degustación 3200 pts + I.V.A.)

Could it be that the Casa del Corregidor's general manager, Máximo Pérez, has a weakness for show-tunes? Why else choose to play *If I Were A Rich Man* in this palatial, Andalucian dining room, which gazes out upon a patchwork countryside across the river below? It would be hard to find any song less appropriate to play in these surroundings. The lush landscape of the Guadalete valley is, in all senses, a long way from the Russian steppe.

In fine weather, you'll sit outside on the terrace, sipping the Parador's complimentary *aperitivo*, overawed by the view. A waitress, a clipped product of the Parador's in-house hotel school and overdressed in ersatz 'national' costume, brings the menu. The *Menú Degustación de la*

Gastronomía de Cádiz comes in the form of a letter on parchment, wax-seal and all, soliciting you most humbly to partake of the Parador's fare. It's tacky as anything—and great fun.

But this is Cádiz province and the *gaditanos* take their food seriously. Of all the provinces of Andalucía, the cuisine of Cádiz is probably the most varied, with its homage to the sea, proximity to the mountains and enduring Moorish legacy. Tarifa, down the road, is after all a mere 16km hop from Tangier.

The menu offers 11 specialities of the region, starting with a grand selection of delectable mountain ham, thick slices of oily orange *chorizo*, and black pudding with nutmeg. *Alcachofas a la algeciraseña*, plump, purple, fleshy artichoke hearts which grow in the sand dunes around Algeciras, are a perfect foil to another dish from the coast, meaty cold-water clams which are definitely Atlantic in size and texture. The Parador has a good policy of serving local wine as well as big Spanish names, and the sepia-whites and tawny-reds of Lebrija and Jerez taste far better than they look.

The muzak flips to *On the Street Where You Live* and an identically clad waitress—distinguishable from her colleague only by a tartan snood—waltzes in with a dish of aubergine baked with black pudding, a wonderful combination of unlikely flavours, and *gazpacho de la tierra en cuenco*, a Moorish-influenced hot *gazpacho* served in earthenware, flavoured with saffron and heavy on the cumin.

Somehow the cassette-tape has lost its way and you may tuck in to your next course to the choral movement of Beethoven's 9th. But it's a fitting accompaniment to the Casa de Corregidor's *pièce-de-résistance*, *urta a la roteña*. Urta is a native of the province, a first cousin of the dentex (a fish which itself sounds remarkably like tooth floss) and a second cousin of the perch. Finned and scaled, it has quite a strong flavour, and cooked *a la roteña*—in the style of Rota, with thyme and brandy—it's a powerful dish, and not for the fainthearted. The music has switched to *Singing in the Rain* and waitress Number One is back, not with an umbrella but a pot of sizzling kidneys in sherry vinegar—pungent lamb's kidneys slightly bitter to the taste.

After a suitable pause—and it's welcome after seven courses—it's time for dessert. These start off with *bizcacho tres gustos de Jerez*, sweetmeats from Jerez, followed by an individual treacle tart and cheese from Grazalema, the last accompanied by a pot of quince jelly.

If all this sounds excessive, it really isn't. The *menú degustación* is intended to let you sample several different dishes of the region, and the size of each portion is quite modest. At any rate, after you have eaten, the waitresses tend to disappear, leaving you on the terrace with a *licor de manzana* or a *brandy de Jerez*, to admire the view or just to doze off. Don't let the jangling notes of *My Favourite Things* or *Hello Dolly!* prevent you.

Urta a la Roteña

(Serves 6–8)

Large urta *or perch, about 1–1.5 kg (2lb 8oz–3lb)*
salt and pepper
flour
6 tablespoons vegetable oil
4 garlic cloves
1 large onion, chopped
2 large red peppers, chopped
4 sprigs of thyme
6 tablespoons brandy
400g/14oz tin of tomatoes, roughly chopped
1 bay leaf
300ml/½ pint light fish stock

Fillet the urta *and make six or eight cutlets by slicing across the fish. Salt and pepper each slice and dredge with flour, shaking off any excess.*

Now heat 4 tablespoons of the oil in a large flameproof casserole, adding the unpeeled garlic. Add the onion and peppers and sauté gently until soft, but do not allow to brown. Now remove the onion, peppers and garlic from the casserole to a warm plate, add the remaining oil and, when it is very hot but not smoking, add the pieces of fish and the thyme, colouring the fish on both sides. After two or three minutes, remove from the heat and add the brandy, then return it to the heat and boil off the brandy.

When the liquid has reduced by about half, add the onion, peppers, tomatoes and bay leaf. Return to a gentle simmer, then add the fish stock and cook over a gentle heat for a further 10 minutes.

Serve with warm pan cateta *and a chilled Lebrija, or a glass of Manzanilla.*

touring around

Madness, interbreeding and witchcraft notwithstanding, there is no more delightful a way to pass a morning or afternoon than meandering through the whitewashed streets of **Arcos de la Frontera**. Apart from the atmosphere of the streets and alleyways themselves, there are a number of buildings of note. The **Plaza de Cabildo** is a handsome rectangular square which serves as a car park. At the southern end, the *mirador* provides the views for which Arcos is justly famous—views of the Guadalete river and the valley beyond. The wheatfields, fruit orchards and vineyards stretch all the way to Jerez.

At the northern end of the square, the 16th-century church of **Santa María** (*open daily 10–1 and 4–7pm*) is a rich architectural mix. The façade fronting the square is plateresque and the interior boasts Gothic, *mudéjar* and Baroque styles, with a fine Renaissance altarpiece. Alongside the church, and opposite the Casa del Corregidor, Arcos's 11th-century Castillo Ducal is still in private hands, still lived in by descendants of the dukes of Arcos.

Leaving the Plaza de Cabildo by the northeast corner, follow the winding streets downhill, passing several *mudéjar palacios*, until you reach the church of **San Pedro** (*open daily 10–1 and 4–7*). This 15th-century church, on the site of an old Arab fortress, is a more florid affair than Santa María. Its interior is rich with Murillos, Zurbaráns and Riberas. The attached bell tower is open to the public between 9am and 2pm and offers a spectacular view.

Arcos de la Frontera

West of the Plaza de Cabildo, the 15th-century **Palacio del Conde del Aguila** and the 16th-century **Palacio Valdespino** can be visited by arrangement with the tourist office in the Ayuntamiento, located opposite the Parador. Look out for the portrait of Charles IV which hangs there—it's attributed to Goya.

Much has been made of the Route of the White Villages, and whilst it would be unfair to say that familiarity breeds contempt, it is worth choosing the villages with care. The C344 between Arcos and Ronda through the Sierra Margarita comes first to **El Bosque**, a rural retreat which boasts Europe's southernmost trout river. From here, the spectacular CA524 descends through the pine forests of the **Parque Natural de la Sierra de Grazalema** to Ubrique, a town of breathtaking appearance—though the reality may disappoint. Its main claim to fame is its manufacture of leather goods.

Now continue on the C3331 for 24km, to **Grazalema** itself. It's a gorgeous town, nestling under the Pico de San Cristobal, and remarkable not least for having the highest rainfall in Spain. It has winding streets, whitewashed houses, and window boxes that provide year-round colour. Three belfries rise from Grazalema's rooftops, while at ground-level the town's good looks are a testament to its wealth derived from the wool trade. Grazalema is definitely worth a detour, but some have found the Junta de Andalucía too assiduous in its task of promoting this particular *pueblo blanco*.

Turn northwards on your loop now, and take the entrancing CA531 to Zahara. This road leads to the **Puerto de las Palomas** (Pass of the Doves), the highest in all Andalucía, and one of the loveliest. **Zahara** itself was declared a National Monument in 1983. Originally settled by the Moors, the town was taken from them by the Christians in 1483. A ruined Moorish castle, a 15th-century church and beautifully preserved cobbled streets make this the most perfect of white villages. From here, cross the Guadalete river back to the C339. Then it's a left turn back to Arcos, or right for the 37km sprint to Ronda.

An excellent excursion south from Arcos is the 35km down the C343 to **Medina Sidonia**. This fortified, hilltop town boasts one of Andalucía's most delightful town squares, the **Plaza Mayor**. Guzmán el Bueno, the town's most famous son, led the Armada against England, and was rewarded with what was to become one of Spain's most noble titles: Duke of Medina Sidonia. There are few tourists and from Medina's ruined castle you can enjoy views to Jerez and Cádiz. If you have been too long in the sierras, the lure of the Atlantic coast may now beckon.

Horses and Courses

Of all Andalucía's small towns, Jerez is perhaps the most complete. It's urbane, sophisticated and totally unprovincial: 2000 years of uninterrupted wine-trade with the rest of the world have seen to that. Even under the 'prohibition' of the Moors, production and trade did not cease.

Where good wine is to be found, good food will follow. And so it's no surprise that Jerez boasts more than its fair share of fine restaurants. On the ground floor of a modern apartment building in a desirable residential neighbourhood, La Mesa Redonda is a gem. Small, discreet and elegantly decorated, this restaurant plays host to cream sherry society. Watch them at work or at play—clinching a deal with a supermarket-chain wine-buyer from the Midwest, or celebrating a talented young *jerezano's* admission to the Andalucian Riding School.

This town lives and breathes sherry—quite literally. In his classic work *Sherry, The Noble Wine* the late Marqués de Bonanza estimated that at any one time there would be

la Mesa Redonda

about 600,000 barrels of the stuff in the town's *bodegas*. That's about 300 million litres. With normal evaporation of at least 5 per cent, that means that every year there's some 15 million litres of wine vapour floating around, to be inhaled by the bibulous *jerezanos*. From whichever direction you hit town, you'll catch it immediately in the air.

Here is a corner of Spain where the British alighted four centuries before they overran the Costas. This was a match made in heaven. For if the Spaniards are rightly disdainful of the English lager-lout, on the rampage in Torremolinos shirtless— and legless—in his Union Jack shorts, in Jerez it's quite another

story. Here an Englishman commands respect still, and *el estilo inglés* is always in fashion. In the *bodegas* which punctuate the town, directors, growers, blenders and tour-guides wear an unofficial uniform to work: grey flannel trousers and hacking jacket. When he dies and goes to heaven, every good *jerezano* prays there will be a branch of Burberry there.

getting there

La Mesa Redonda is located in a residential precinct off the Avenida Alcalde Álvaro Domecq, about 1.5km from the centre of town. From the centre, follow signs for the Museo de los Relojes and Real Escuela Andaluza de Arte Ecuestre. These signs will bring you to the Plaza Marmelón. Now follow signs for the Royal Sherry Park Hotel, leaving the square by the street at the northeast corner, Avenida Sevilla. This street becomes Alcalde Álvaro Domecq. Continue for about 250m until you see the Sherry Park on your left. The precinct which houses La Mesa Redonda will now be opposite, on your right-hand side, behind the bus stop. It's tricky to spot from the road, so the Sherry Park is your best landmark.

La Mesa Redonda

Manuel de la Quintana 3, Jerez, ℂ (95) 634 0069. Closed Sun. Booking advisable, essential Thurs lunch. 4000–5000 pts.

This beautifully furnished restaurant, owned by Margarita de Carrixosa and her husband José Antonio Valdespino, is all high-born elegance. Once behind the discreetly located front door, you can take in the restaurant at a glance—it's not a big place. At the front is a comfortable, old-fashioned sitting area with deep sofas and, in the handsome bookcases, a culinary library. Old classic volumes juxtaposed with new—reference works which have stood the test of time alongside trendy, nine-day's wonders—tell a story. Here's a restaurant that knows all the rules, but is confident enough to re-interpret them.

After introductions have been made, Margarita will offer you a drink in the small sitting area or, should you prefer, take you directly to your table. There are only a dozen or so, impeccably dressed with gleaming glass and silver—and the chairs are the most comfortable in southern Spain. As for an *aperitivo*, while the choice of sherries is obviously extensive, if sherry isn't your drink, feel free to digress. Just as European chefs choose Chinese food when they're having a night off, it seems that the first thing a *bodega* boss does when he's out of his office is to order a large gin and tonic.

José Antonio runs a superb kitchen at La Mesa Redonda. His dishes have a rare quality of being up-front and gutsy, while still looking wonderful on the plate. *Ghistorras picantes*, hot red sausages, are fiery indeed, yet the heat doesn't mask the flavour; *setas al amontillado*, wild mushrooms in a rich, reduced sherry sauce are truly 'wild'; while the *ensalada al vinagre de Jerez* takes the finest local ingredients—and these may change daily—such as Jabugo ham and white asparagus, and combines them with a vinaigrette that tastes like no other.

In autumn and winter, the menu may be supplemented with game: pheasant, partridge, woodcock and snipe on a good day. José Antonio roasts these in a traditional way, or may poach them in a sherry sauce. From the regular menu, fish dishes include *hojaldre de rape y gambas*, a *millefeuille* of monkfish and prawns; and *salmón a la pimienta rosa*, juicy, local wild salmon with a pink pepper sauce.

Like the starters, the meat dishes are feisty and flavoursome, such as *solomillo de buey al oloroso*, a succulent fillet steak with sweet sherry; or *muslo de pato al solera*, a confit of duck in a concentrated, caramelly sherry sauce; or another wonderful duck dish, *magret de pato en amontillado con mermelada de cebolla*— duck breast in Amontillado sherry with onion marmalade.

These dishes call for big wines, which you'll find in plentiful supply. For a white wine, consider something local—this is, after all, the home of the unique *albarizo* chalky white soil, and the Palomino grape it produces. For a red, perhaps the *Marqués de Arienzo* 1990, a perfectly balanced wine from Elciego in the heart of La Rioja. Best of all, ask Margarita. Her knowledge of wines is encyclopaedic and she will happily advise you in her beautiful and fluent English.

Desserts range from the simple to the elaborate. After a rich lunch, an elegantly presented bowl of fresh fruit may be just the ticket. On the other hand, the kitchen's *pièce de résistance*, a white and dark chocolate mousse, may be harder to resist than Jerez's famous pudding, *tocino de cielo*, an over-sweet caramel custard which translates literally as 'heaven's bacon'. One wonders how the hacking jackets can possibly go back to work at 5pm after a lunch such as this—but they do. After 500 years in Jerez, the British still have much to learn.

Frances Bissell, the *Times* cook, is a great fan of La Mesa Redonda. A letter from her and her husband to Margarita and José Antonio, framed on the wall at the entrance, pays testament: 'How lucky for us that you were at home!... Both of us remarked on how each time we taste José Antonio's food it just gets better and better. It has always been marvellous—but now it's in a very special class.' There are many who share their opinion.

Riñones al Jerez

This classic dish of Jerez is as impressive to eat as it is easy to make. Although it cannot be made in advance, the speed and simplicity of its preparation makes it ideal nevertheless for a sophisticated supper party or a special dîner-à-deux.

(Serves 2–4)

8 lambs' kidneys
4 tablespoons vegetable oil
200ml/7fl oz medium sherry
75g/3oz unsalted butter
2 tablespoons plain flour
400ml/14fl oz chicken stock
salt and pepper

Wash and thoroughly clean the kidneys in several changes of water. Heat the oil in a frying pan and sauté the kidneys for two or three minutes, so they just firm up enough to slice easily. Now, remove the kidneys, drain off the excess oil and, using a very sharp knife, slice them thinly, as you would a mushroom. Arrange the slices in a flameproof casserole, pour over the sherry and cook for a further two minutes over a medium heat.

Meanwhile, in a small saucepan, make a roux by melting the butter, stirring in the flour, cooking it for a minute or two, then gradually adding the chicken stock, stirring all the time. As soon as it is smooth and foaming, add it to the casserole, season with salt and a few twists of the pepper mill and cook for a further minute, until all the ingredients have combined. Serve immediately.

touring around

Jerez de la Frontera is a smallish town which you can comfortably cover in a day: a sherry *bodega* in the morning, a stroll around the Clock Museum and the shopping streets in the afternoon. Jerez is eminently manageable. That said, there are some sights which many would consider too good to miss. Opening hours are bizarre and a visit to Jerez may require careful planning.

First, try to come on a Thursday. This is the day—the *only* day of the week—when the riders of the Spanish Riding School perform their remarkable equine display at **La Real Escuela Andaluza de Arte Ecuestre**, located one block northwest of La Mesa Redonda on the Avenida Duque de Abrantes. The show, in a pint-sized modern arena, is a kind of showjumping-meets-*Swan Lake*, a marvellous equine ballet set to music. Kick-off is at 12 sharp; tickets cost from 1750 pts and are available at the ticket windows on the day, or may be reserved in advance by telephone, ✆ (95) 631 1111. The school is open on other days between 11am and 1.30pm, when for 450 pts you may wander round the stables and admire the comfort in which these pampered creatures live. By the way, if you come in winter, wear some warm clothes: the arena is unheated and, regardless of the outside temperature, it can feel very cold inside.

A tour of a sherry ***bodega*** certainly holds its own with a tour around a winery in, say, France or the USA. The British have enjoyed sherry since the 15th century, and even today, with 90 per cent of Spanish sherry production reserved for export, it is the British who consume 40 per cent of it. The mysteries of this complex wine will be unlocked as you walk around the *bodega,* following the course of the Palomino grape through harvesting, sun-drying and pressing to its fortification with alcohol, after which it enters the *solera,* a system of 'topping up' the sherry, actually blending the new with the old to produce a consistent, 'non-vintage' wine. The great *bodegas,* Harveys ✆ (95) 615

1030, Domecq ☎ (95) 633 1800, Sandeman ☎ (95) 630 1100, Williams & Humbert ☎ (95) 633 1300 and González Byass ☎ (95) 634 0000, were, or still are, part-British owned and are familiar names in the UK. All have extensive grounds and gardens (beware of the alligator at Harveys) and all offer some kind of tour, although these vary according to demand. It's best to phone for details and to reserve your place—most charge for the tour but the ticket price is negligible (about 300 pts), especially when weighed against the numerous 'free samples' you will taste as the tour proceeds. If you're planning to come to Jerez for the Thursday horse show, you'll need a *bodega* tour which starts early: **González Byass** usually has one at 9.30. If you're late and have to join the 10am group you'll be in for a surprise: it's conducted entirely in Japanese.

Other sights of the town include the **Museo Atalaya de Relojes**, (clock museum) in Calle Cervantes, ☎ (95) 618 2100 (*open Mon–Sat 10–1.30; adm*), a fascinating collection of predominantly British and French 18th- and 19th-century timepieces.

A block south of Jerez's main square, the **Plaza del Arenal**, lies the 11th-century **Alcázar** (*open Mon–Fri 10.30–2, 4.30–7; Sat 10–1.30; adm free*). It contains a mosque, later converted into a church (**Santa María la Real**), the **Torre Octagonal**, a Moorish octagonal tower, and the **Baños Arabes**, the Arabic baths. Two blocks to the east, opposite the Tourist Office, the *mudéjar* and Gothic **Convento de Santo Domingo** (*open Mon–Fri 10–1 and 4–8*), gutted in the Civil War but carefully restored, is well worth a visit. Jerez's Baroque **Catedral de San Salvador** or **La Colegiata** (*open Mon–Sat 10–8; Sun 11–2 and 6–8; adm free*) is impressive, if somewhat overpowering, built on the site of an Arab mosque. Opposite the cathedral is the **Barrio de Santiago**, Jerez's gipsy quarter. It is known for its four churches dedicated to the Evangelists, Matthew, Mark, Luke and John. The Barrio is a delightful part of town for an early-evening stroll.

If *ferias* are to your liking, those of Jerez are enormous fun. In early May the *Feria del Caballo* is a horse fair like no other, with dressage, carriage-driving and races featuring the town's famous *Cartujana* (Carthusian) horses. The town's other obsession is fêted in September: the wine harvest celebrations are possibly the best in Spain.

Columbus, Vespucci and the Sea-salt Tang of Manzanilla

Paco Secundino

In a magnificent position at the mouth of the Guadalquivir river, Sanlúcar de Barrameda, along with Jerez and El Puerto de Santa María, makes up the third town of the sherry triumvirate.

In character, she could not be more different from her relations. Homely, poorly dressed and impervious to what the neighbours think, she is blessed with an enormous sense of fun. Sanlúcar's summer months are filled with *ferias* which celebrate the things closest to her heart: in May, the Feria de la

Manzanilla, when the streets are awash with alcohol; in June, Corpus Christi with fireworks; and in August, six days of horse-racing along the beach—an annual event that's gone on uninterrupted for the last 150 years. Oh, and let's not forget the Festival de la Exaltación del Rio Guadalquivir, another August event, when homage is paid to the river which brought this town to prominence, in a week-long celebration with flamenco, street dances and bullfighting.

A hundred years ago, Sanlúcar was southern Spain's most popular resort. Down on the beach at Bajo de Guía, it's not hard to imagine Spaniards of a bygone era taking a *paseo* along the promenade in their stiff and formal costumes. The seafront still has an old-fashioned air about it—earnest young boys playing football with proud grandfathers looking on, and fishermen mending their nets.

The line of restaurants facing the beach is daunting. Some are well-known and feature in every guide; some are family-run; some tout for your trade. Nearly all are good—it's difficult not to be when the fish is landed outside your door.

If you have your favourite, so be it. If not, head for Paco Secundino. Fifty years in the business may just have given him an edge over his competitors. At any event, this is a lunch and a setting you'll be unlikely to forget.

getting there

The restaurant is located on the wide beach and promenade known as Bajo de Guía, at the eastern end of the town.

Approaching Sanlúcar from Jerez and Sevilla, follow the yellow 'hotel' signs for Hotel Doñana and Bajo de Guía. This route takes you around the outskirts of the town in an anti-clockwise direction along the Avenida de la Constitución, with a fine view of the *bodega* rooftops as you descend to the lower part of town. At the T-junction, turn right on to the Avenida de Bajo de Guía, and carry on until just before the road ends in a roundabout: this strip is the

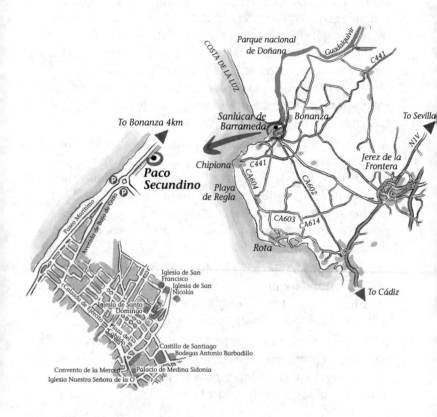

car park for the beach. It's walking only from here. Secundino is the fifth restaurant along the esplanande.

From Chipiona, descend through the middle of Sanlúcar, following signs for the central Plaza del Cabildo, then continue downhill along Sanlúcar's impressive *rambla*, the Calzada de Ejército. After 300m, turn right on to the Avenida de Bajo de Guía and continue as above. (If you miss this turning and continue on to the beach, no matter. Turn right onto the Paseo Marítimo which rejoins the Avenida de Bajo de Guía after a few hundred metres.)

Paco Secundino

Bajo de Guía s/n, Sanlúcar de Barrameda (Cádiz), © (95) 636 6884. Open daily. About 3500–4000 pts.

The plastic chairs are a bit rickety and the interior could do with a facelift. In short, everything is just as it should be in this wholly unpretentious seafood restaurant. If the weather is half decent—and with 320 days of sunshine a year in the region, it should be—tables will be laid up outside. Dogs, footballs and small boys are an occupational hazard of eating on the esplanade, but a small price to pay for the sea air and the views across the wide, wide River Guadalquivir to the Coto Doñana nature reserve on the opposite shore.

Sanlúcar is the home of Manzanilla, the sherry with a 'sea-salt' tang. This is usually put down to the salt content in the soil, and the *poniente* wind which blows—saltily—across the Coto Doñana from the ocean. There's no point in ordering a glass, or *copita*: here in Sanlúcar, it's bottles and half-bottles only. As a mark of how seriously the drink is taken, the waiter will lug a free-standing ice-bucket out onto the esplanade and set it beside your table. Manzanilla needs to be drunk very cold.

A look at the display inside the restaurant may help you order, or merely identify the fish and shellfish you see on the menu. *Almejas*, big juicy clams, are reminiscent of their East Coast American counterparts. Try these clams marinated or grilled—either way they're delicious—while a *cocktail de marisco* (plump, juicy prawns hauled out of the sea a few hours earlier, and topped with a paprika-spiked *Marie-Rose* sauce) gives quite a new perspective to the dreary lettuce-bound prawn cocktail so beloved of the English.

Like most informal restaurants in Spain, there's no need to order two courses at the beginning of the meal. Take time over your starter, enjoy the wonderful view—the busy waterfront has a distinctly African feel to it here in Bajo de Guía—and down another glass of Manzanilla before deciding what to eat next. Waiters are usually very accommodating with this kind of 'fits and starts' ordering.

When you're ready, move into the serious *mariscos*. There may be *langostas*, spiny lobster, or *cigalas*, red and meaty Dublin Bay prawns, or *bogavante*, maritime Cádiz province's medium-sized lobster. All are served *a la plancha*, grilled over a hot iron plate and served with lemon and mayonnaise. There's usually a dazzling display of other *pescados* too, such as *rape* (angler fish, more refined perhaps in a *brocheta* than the over-sauced *cazuela* (stew)); *marrajo*, a juicy shark fillet; delectable *pijotas fritas* (fried baby hake); *salmonetes o sardinas a la parrilla* (red mullet or sardines on a skewer) and our old friend the *urta* (sea-bream), now just a stone's-throw away from his native Rota.

Out in the open air, especially in the winter months when the sun and blue sky belie a chilly temperature, you'll find the first half-bottle of Manzanilla soon becomes a second. No words of comfort here: it's powerful stuff which, enjoyed at lunchtime, can seriously affect afternoon plans. Given this, you might enjoy instead some of Barbadillo's local wines, such as the '93 *Castillo Espiritu Santu*, a Chablis-like big white made, like sherry itself, from the Palomino grape.

As for desserts, they might seem almost superfluous after these subtle seafood flavours, but a sugary *tocino de cielo*, Jerez's famous pudding, may be a good antidote to the salty Manzanilla.

When you have finished eating, take a stroll along the esplanade to the end of Bajo de Guía, and muse on Columbus (on his second voyage) and Amerigo Vespucci setting sail for the New World from these waters 500 years ago. It's a romantic thought.

On the way back, you can always stop at your table for another cup of coffee and a pick-me-up *refresco*. The pace is unhurried in this town: the chances are that the waiter won't have cleared your table yet, nor even have realized you had gone.

Pijotas Fritas

Málaga and Cádiz are both known for their frituras. *This platter of freshly caught, freshly fried fish is one of the great culinary experiences of the South. Away from the coast, you can't hope to reproduce a* fritura *in its entirety, but with choice ingredients, such as chunky* merluza *(hake) or, as we use here,* pijota *(baby hake), you will nevertheless be able to recreate part of this wonderful taste sensation.*

(Serves 6)

1kg/2¼ lbs filleted hake, cut into bite-sized pieces or goujons
600ml/1 pint milk
flour, for coating
600ml/1 pint vegetable or groundnut oil
salt and pepper
3 lemons, each cut in half
mayonnaise, to serve (preferably homemade)

In a shallow dish, soak the goujons *of hake in the milk for 15 minutes.*
Shake some plain flour evenly over a baking tray and coat the pieces of fish
with it, shaking off the excess. In a large, heavy-based frying pan, heat the
oil. When it is very hot, drop in the fish and fry for 2 or 3 minutes on each
side, until crisp and golden. Sprinkle with salt to taste, a few twists of the
pepper mill, and serve piping hot with the lemon halves and mayonnaise.

touring around

The shabby, peeling town of **Sanlúcar de Barrameda**, with very few
exceptions, has yet to fall prey to the restorers—and therein lies its
appeal. Like Jerez, it's best seen on foot: most of its fine buildings and
historic monuments lie in the **Barrio Alto** (upper part of town),
within striking distance of the **Plaza del Cabildo**. Start your walka-
bout in this lovely central square.

South of the square, across Calle Anche, lies another handsome
square, **Plaza de San Roque**, and by continuing diagonally across this
square and along **Bretones** you come to the 17th-century **Convento
de la Merced** and the 19th-century **Montpensier Palace** (*open
Mon–Sat 9–1.30*), with an extensive library and paintings by Murillo,
El Greco, Rubens and Goya. Carry on up this hill and turn left at the
end. This will bring you to Sanlúcar's most imposing (and restored)
church of **Nuestra Señora de la O**, started in the 13th-century, originally completed in the 14th, and much added-to since.

The church leads directly into the **Palacio de Medina Sidonia**, occupied until recently by the outspoken Duchess of Medina Sidonia,
direct descendant of Guzmán el Bueno (*see* p.137), a radical aristocrat
and champion of the poor. Parts of the palace may be visited by
appointment, ✆ (95) 636 0161. Continuing east from **Nuestra Señora**

de la O, carry on past the impressive Moorish **Castillo de Santiago**, now a ruin, until you reach the *bodega* of **Antonio Barbadillo**, the town's biggest producer of Manzanilla. The *bodega* is open for visits Monday to Fridays, mornings only (*✆ (95) 636 5103 for further information and to reserve places on a tour.*)

From the back of the castle, take the steps connecting the **Barrio Alto** with the **Barrio Bajo** below. It will bring you close to a cluster of three churches: the Renaissance **Iglesia de Santo Domingo**, with its vaulted ceiling stone-built 16th-century convent; the **Iglesia de San Nicolás**; and the **Iglesia de San Francisco**, built by Henry VIII during his marriage to Catherine of Aragon as a hospital for British sailors.

Across the river from Bajo de Guía, the magnificent **Coto Doñana nature reserve**, at the edge of the **Parque Nacional de Doñana**, probably Europe's largest wildlife sanctuary, is the perfect place to spend what's left of the afternoon once you have finished lunch, taking in one of Sanlúcar's famous sunsets on the return crossing. Unfortunately, access is not particularly easy and, although motor boats do ply for trade across the river, you won't get to see much of the reserve unless you join an organized tour. These can be arranged in town through **Tourafrica**, Calle San Juan 8, *✆ (95) 636 2540*.

Another way to amuse yourself after lunch—if you can stand yet more fish—is to visit the public fish auction in **Bonanza**, 4km away.

Leaving Sanlúcar to the south, **Chipiona** is a family summer resort, full of small *pensiones*, with a good beach at **Playa de Regla** near the lighthouse. Next, on the edge of the bay of Cádiz, comes **Rota**, a bigger, flashier resort taking advantage of the best and longest beach on this part of the coast. The town is pretty, though a bit overbuilt. It's also full of Americans from one of Europe's largest naval bases, 250sq km of it, just outside town. This was the key base Franco gave up in the 1953 deal with President Eisenhower. In the recent dealings over the future of Spain's role in NATO, the Americans made it clear that this base is not a subject for negotiation, while in the 1986 NATO referendum this region turned out the highest 'yes' vote in Spain.

In the bars and fast food joints of Sanlúcar, El Puerto de Santa Maria and Cádiz, it's strange to behold strapping marines down bottles of Spanish beer—as if Columbus's chickens have come home to roost.

The Women in Black

Strung out in a loose curve on a high ridge between sea and mountains, the first glimpse of Vejer de la Frontera from the main N340 highway is dramatic. Jan Morris calls it 'perhaps the most spectacular of Spanish villages': it would be hard to argue.

Vejer has it all. It's not just its whitewashed alleys, its wrought-iron *rejas* (grilles) or its balconies covered with flowering geraniums; in Andalucía, even the most romantic traveller will soon come to take these classic components in his stride. Vejer offers a more profound look at the soul of Andalucía, encapsulated in a few snatched, plaintive bars of a gipsy's song or the cosy smell of a freshly-baked *cholla* (Jewish loaf). The song, like the *cholla* recipe, is over a thousand years old, but neither the gipsy nor the baker concerns himself with that.

Until the 1970s, many of the women of Vejer wore traditional dress: a long, black tunic or *cobijada* which covered them from head to toe, with a veil for the face which left only one eye

La Posada

uncovered. Occasionally the women dress up still, more in the interests of tourism than to fulfil a tradition, but the effect is macabre nevertheless.

Arrive on a summer's afternoon and you'll think you've found a ghost-town, blinds drawn, shutters barred against a relentless, unforgiving sun. Come in the midst of winter, when the rain whips in from the Atlantic and can lash the town for a fortnight without stopping, and you'll want to turn heel and flee. But the chances are that you'll get it right and then Vejer will reveal at least some of her mysteries to you.

The town is a perfect base for some gentle, local exploration. The San Francisco, a former convent which now serves as one of the town's very few hotels, is a popular if dreary place

where your bedroom is a converted nun's cell and you wouldn't be in the least surprised to have Mother Superior at the front desk do a bell-book-and-candle routine on you if you dared to complain.

Around the corner and down the hill, La Posada, with its local busybodies and hangers-on clustered round the bar, seems to pick up on the mood of Vejer. The *tapas* are freshly prepared throughout the day, the conversation is animated, and a long, late lunch rolls effortlessly on until the sun is well past the Bay of Cádiz.

You may not eat like a caliph at La Posada but you will certainly eat like a *hidalgo*. You'll be treated like one too, which is better still.

getting there

Vejer de la Frontera is easily reached from the N340 Costa de la Luz/Costa del Sol coastal highway. Approximately halfway between Cádiz and Algeciras, turn off the N340 at the Vejer sign on to a road which winds a scenic 4km into town.

La Posada is located on a straight, uphill slope on the right-hand side of this road, as it nears the centre of Vejer. The restaurant faces the long esplanade, with its marvellous views down to the coast.

Coming from Barbate, take the C343 to Vejer (10km). Continue around the town following signs for Cádiz and Algeciras. You will find La Posada on your left-hand side on the straight, downhill slope as you leave the centre of the town.

La Posada

Avenida de los Remedios 19, Vejer de la Frontera (Cádiz), © (95) 645 0111. Open daily 1–5 and 8–11. About 3000 pts.

A lattice partition separates the main restaurant from a gleaming *tapas* bar. In the restaurant proper, white tablecloths over pink undercloths, and starched linen napkins standing to attention, oak beams and iron chandeliers give the appearance of a far grander establishment than La Posada really is.

The charming and helpful waiter will show you to a table and take your order for drinks. *Tinto de verano*, a summer cup of wine and lemonade, makes a light, refreshing *aperitivo*, and you can drink it throughout lunch. On the other hand, the locally bottled house wine, *Viña Celia*, is too good to pass up at 500 pts a bottle.

First courses at La Posada include cured loin of pork and Jabugo ham, while locally caught clams find their way into an excellent *almejas a la marinera*, clams 'marinière'. Another alternative is to choose your starter from the *tapas* bar—down two steps to where a big selection of hors d'œuvre awaits, with dishes such as quail's eggs, mussels, anchovies in vinegar, red-pepper salad and spicy meatballs.

Main courses are for the most part simple, their strength lying in the use of excellent local produce. Fish comes in daily from the fishing villages below Vejer. In the chilled display cabinet you may see *parga*, 'porgy' (a kind of sea-bream), which La Posada serves with clams in a white wine sauce; or a couple of *salmonetes* (red mullet) may give you the wink. *Atún*, the tuna for which these coastal waters were once famous, is now more scarce, but if it's on the menu take advantage—plain grilled, with a rich homemade mayonnaise, or baked with garlic and tomatoes.

Meat dishes are seasonal too: partridge or pheasant in a hearty winter stew and, in the spring, *chuletillas de cordero*, lamb cutlets so small and sweet and young it seems almost wrong to eat them.

The good news is that there's no need to save room for dessert: they're the usual Andalucian let-down from the freezer, save for a decent custard and a homemade *crema catalana*. Instead, mellow out to an entrancing Spanish cover version of Elton John's Greatest Hits, and move straight on to coffee and a shot of *licor dulce*, before setting forth to discover Vejer.

Atún con Tomate y Aceitunas

Fresh tuna is a wonderfully flavoursome fish, and bears little or no resemblance to the stuff that comes out of tins. Try to find a fishmonger who will cut fillets from a very big fish—the larger the steaks, the better the texture and flavour. The subtlety of this dish—tuna baked with tomatoes and olives—belies the speed and ease with which it can be prepared.

(Serves 4)

8 tablespoons olive oil
2 cloves of garlic, crushed
pinch of dried oregano
juice of 2 lemons
4 tuna steak fillets, about 175g/6oz each
flour
200ml/7fl oz medium-dry white wine
450g/1lb peeled plum tomatoes, roughly chopped
200g/7oz anchovy-stuffed green olives
1 bay leaf

Preheat the oven to 180°C/350°F (gas mark 4). Combine the olive oil, garlic, oregano and lemon juice in a large bowl and marinate the tuna in this mixture for ten minutes or so. Then remove, reserving the marinade, and dredge the tuna steaks with flour, shaking off the excess. Now heat the reserved marinade in a large ovenproof casserole and quickly brown the tuna over a medium-high heat. After a couple of minutes on each side, turn up the heat and add the white wine, letting it boil for two to three minutes.

Remove the tuna and transfer to a warm dish. Now turn the heat back to medium and add the tomatoes along with the olives and bay leaf. When this is simmering, return the tuna to the casserole and bake in the oven for 10 to 15 minutes, but no longer as the fish dries out very quickly. Serve immediately.

touring around

Lazy sightseers will love exploring **Vejer de la Frontera**. While it does have some buildings of note, its charms lie chiefly in the atmosphere of its whitewashed streets and alleyways, where every aspect pleases. From La Posada, turn right onto Los Remedios and then right again into the Plazuela. Just off this square you will find the tourist office, where you can arm yourself with a good map of the *pueblo*. (If the tourist office is closed—opening times are somewhat erratic—the San Francisco Convent hotel, also off the square, might oblige.)

The two main landmarks of Vejer are the **Iglesia del Divino Salvador** (*open usually Mon–Sat 11–1.30 and Mon–Fri 6–8*), with its mixture of Romanesque, *mudéjar* and Gothic styles—so something for everyone there—and the **Castillo Moro** (*open daily 10–2 and also 4.30–8.30 in high season*), where you can walk along the battlements and enjoy a ravishing view of Vejer. In the upper part of town, look out for several original Moorish arches. And in case you're in need of further refreshment, in the Bar Chirino on the Plaza España there's a fascinating collection of old photographs of the town.

Vejer is situated about halfway between Cádiz and Algeciras, a few kilometres inland from Spain's last great undiscovered coast, the **Costa de la Luz**. At the moment, the area (with the exception of

Tarifa) attracts mainly Spaniards, and only in high season. Except in June, July and August, the beaches are largely deserted. However, with the Costa del Sol's continued westward expansion, the improved highway between Algeciras and Málaga, and Sevilla's underused airport looking for business, it can only be a matter of time before the developers move in to the Atlantic beaches of southern Spain.

From Vejer the C343 goes down to the modern town of **Barbate** (or Barbate de Franco to give it its full name), whose income comes not from tourists but from tuna. Twice a year shoals of tuna pass by here, to be thwarted in a bloody ambush. But the size of the shoals is dwindling, probably due to extensive overfishing. This is yet another reason why the area is looking to tourism to balance its books.

A small road leads west out of Barbate to the summer resort of **Los Caños de Meca**. Traditionally busy in the height of summer with tourists from Sevilla and Cádiz, recent years have seen hordes of Germans adopt the place as their escape haven. Half-an-hour's walk west of here takes you to **Cape Trafalgar**, where Nelson breathed his last in 1805. Spaniards remember this well; it was mostly their ships that were getting smashed, under incompetent French leadership. Every Spaniard did his duty, though, and with their unflappable sense of personal honour the Spanish have always looked on Trafalgar as a sort of victory.

Some 10km south of here is another developing resort, **Zahara de los Atunes** ('of the tunas'). The town was the birthplace of Francisco Rivera, or Paquirri, the famous bullfighter.

Tarifa, at the southwestern tip of Spain and of Europe, has the quality of looking either exotic and evocative, or merely dusty and dreary, depending on the mood you're in and the hour of the day. You might even think you've arrived in Africa, it's so bleached by sun and salt. The town is one of the top destinations in Europe for the masters of the art of windsurfing; the *levante* and *poniente* winds are relentless in their attack on this coast. There are miles of beaches around to choose from. The town has a 10th-century Moorish **castle**, much rebuilt since. As every Spanish schoolboy knows—or used to know—this is the site of the legend of Guzmán el Bueno. In 1292 this Spanish knight was defending Tarifa against a force of Moors. Among them was the renegade Infante Don Juan, brother of King Sancho IV, who had Guzmán's young son as a prisoner, and threatened to kill him if Guzmán did not surrender. Guzmán's response was to toss him a dagger. His son was killed, but Tarifa did not fall.

And on that cheerful note, you too must make a choice; to stay on Spain's Atlantic coast or continue on. For it's here at Tarifa that the Atlantic meets the Mediterranean, and Europe and Africa all but touch. It's a romantic spot, especially at sunset on Tarifa's ramparts, where you can watch the sun slip slowly into the ocean.

Langostas and *Gambas* at the Foot of the Rock

Ten minutes from the polo fields and manicured lawns of Sotogrande, you'll find yourself in La Línea. The contrast could not be more acute. Here are the mean streets of Spain, a crumbling, poor, urban wasteland where boys and old men stand idly around on street corners looking for anything to relieve the boredom, and fires blaze on building sites and roadside rubbish tips. Who starts them, and who puts them out—for the authorities do not seem much in evidence in anarchic La Línea—is anybody's guess.

And there at the end of the town, a backdrop to this human opera, looms the Rock of Gibraltar, immense, ugly, in total disharmony with its surroundings, yet coloured so richly with the paint-palette of history.

Gibraltar and La Línea are inseparable entities, their stories so entwined, living—as they've always done—in each other's pockets. Until Franco closed the border in 1969, residents of La Línea would cross the frontier daily to go to work in Gib. Now the gates are open, but there's no longer work to be had.

La Marina

There's always smuggling, of course. With cigarettes at 60p a packet in Gibraltar, there are handsome profits to be made for the price of a motorboat and a bit of nerve.

Gibraltar and La Línea's home-reared smugglers buy goods in Gibraltar, then speed along the shore, literally throwing the contraband to their colleagues waiting on the La Línea beach—cheered on by a crowd of onlookers only too happy to give the signal should the Customs police decide to put in an appearance. The cartons of cut-priced Marlboro and Winston you're offered at traffic lights the length and breadth of Spain have usually entered the country by way of La Línea's beach.

Like all underprivileged areas in Spain, lottery-ticket vendors abound. These men and women seem to harbour in their troubled faces a lifetime of experience. When you buy a ticket and they smile and wish you ¡Que tengas suerte!—good luck—your heart will give a little leap. In La Línea, *tapas* bars, too, abound—and the *tapas* are tangy and delicious, piled high and sold cheap. Any other way and it just wouldn't wash here. If La Línea can be said to have a high-point, then it is surely its food. It's more than can be said for Gibraltar which certainly cannot number food amongst its attractions. If you're visiting the Rock, be smart—plan your itinerary around lunch in La Línea.

The mile-long Paseo Marítimo, La Línea's seaside promenade along its eastern flank, seethes with activity. In the middle of it all, in a modern, low slung concrete cabin plonked down on the beach circa 1966 and still curiously out of place, is La Marina. It looks more like a particularly corrupt government department than a restaurant—but restaurant it most certainly is. Stolid, confident and a trifle arrogant too, La Marina is a La Línea institution. And don't worry about parking your car outside, even though the street could not look less friendly if it tried. La Marina's parking attendant will guard it with his life.

getting there

Approaching La Línea from the east (Costa del Sol) on the N340, take the first turning signposted La Línea/Gibraltar via a filter lane off to the left. This road, the CA233, makes a spectacular descent into La Línea, with superb views of Gibraltar in the distance.

Follow this road through the outskirts of La Línea until you come to a set of traffic lights at the Shell garage. Turn left at these lights (you'll need to get into the left-hand filter lane). Continue along this road for about 1km, through two sets of defunct traffic lights, until it swings round to the right to bring you to the Paseo Marítimo. La Marina restaurant is located about 300m further on, on the sea-side of this road.

From the Costa de la Luz and Algeciras on the N340, follow signs for La Línea/Gibraltar, turning right on to the N351. This road takes you through El Campamento to approach La Línea from the west. Continue to follow signs to Gibraltar (this will save you having to negotiate the centre of La Línea), all the way to the frontier. If you find yourself in a long line of traffic as you near the

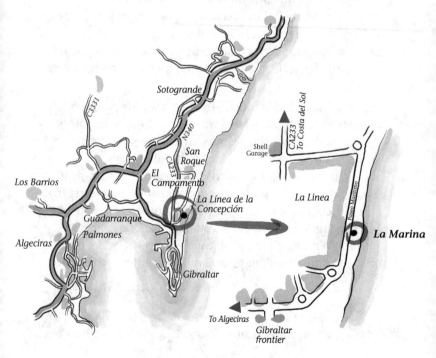

Langostas *and* Gambas *at the Foot of the Rock*

frontier, you can overtake the lot in the offside lane—they're
queuing to get into Gib.

Continue past the frontier gates as far as you can go, turning left at
the end of the road where you are obliged to do so. Continue over
two very big, deserted roundabouts, keeping the sea as close to you
as possible, on your right. La Marina is located 300m on your
right, after the second roundabout.

La Marina

*La Atunara, Paseo Marítimo s/n, 11300 La Línea de la Concepción
(Cádiz), ✆ (95) 610 1531, ✆ (95) 676 9606. Open daily. About 4000 pts.*

Step inside La Marina and the view will knock you for six. There,
through the restaurant's huge, plate-glass windows, the Rock of
Gibraltar is staring you in the face. Can it be real? You can almost
touch it. Out at sea, stacked like counters of a child's board game, oil
tankers, NATO aircraft-carriers and maybe the odd warship jockey for
position, in the lee of Gibraltar's calm, Mediterranean shore.

The first of La Marina's four adjoining dining rooms is itself a *tapas*
bar, decorated with nice old tiles and some fascinating black-and-
white and sepia photographs of La Línea and Gibraltar at the turn of
the century. You could start off at the bar with a *ración* of *pulpo*
(octopus) to share, or a plate of *boquerones al vinagre*, anchovies in
vinegar, washed down with an ice-cold beer or glass of *fino*.
For most, the pull of the view will be too great and you'll
want to sit down at your table right away. Don't forget to
check out the piscatorial display and the lobster tank, as
you head into the main dining room. And insist on the
table of your choice—don't be fobbed off with any second-
rate table if a first-rate one by the window seems to be free.

A white-jacketed waiter will bring you a menu—probably in
English. With that rather irritating sixth sense that waiters have, he
knows you're not local even before you open your mouth. Well,
there's nothing wrong with an English menu, as long as it's intelli-
gible; however you might actually find the Spanish easier to
understand!

To start, why not choose some dishes from the section titled *Platos Para Picar*—dishes to nibble at: *ensalada de pimientos asados*, a delicious salad of roasted red peppers; *surtidos de conchas gratinadas*, a selection of mussels, clams, sea-urchins—whatever the catch has brought in—*au gratin*; *tortillitas de camarones*, piping-hot fritters of shrimp, like a giant prawn-cracker; or *croquetitas de bacalao*, croquettes of salt-cod which taste a whole lot better than they sound.

Main courses are, of course, fishy, and vary daily according to the market. *Langostas*, lobsters, tend usually to be small in the winter months, but it's quality, not quantity which counts. Have them plain grilled with a good squeeze of lemon—their succulent sweetness is superb. *Navajas*, grilled razor clams, are another unusual shellfish which are a real treat, so too the *gambas pil-pil*, meaty prawns liberally spiked with paprika and garlic and served sizzling in an earthenware dish. Other fish dishes might include *besugo al aliño marinero*, sea-bream served *à la marinière*; *mero a la Navarra*, grouper stuffed with ham; or *salmonetes* (red mullet) or *pez espada* (swordfish) cooked on the griddle. And unusually for this part of the world, La Marina offers some vegetable dishes too, such as *panaché de verduras frescas al aceite de oliva virgen*, a selection of mostly green vegetables served warm with a swirl of olive oil; *palmitos al Roquefort*, hearts of palm with Roquefort dressing, and *habitas con jamon*, baby broad beans with cubes of ham.

La Marina has an interesting wine list with some young wines from Huelva and Cádiz, although you may fare better with something more substantial from the north. The house white, *Don Darias*, a favourite along Spain's southern coast, is very drinkable and unbeatable value at 700 pts.

Desserts, the poor relation in Andalucía's restaurants, are eminently missable, though if you need a sugar-fix there's the usual *flan*, custards, rice pudding, as well as some homemade sponge cakes and sweet meringues.

Your fellow diners at La Marina are an eclectic bunch. Businessmen or oilmen from the refineries at San Roque; a couple of Gibraltar lawyers thrashing out a contract over lunch; a pair of local sweethearts; and perhaps even a table of English matrons down from Gaucín, with grey hair and sensible shoes. They've lived around here for ever of course, long before the present generation of *arrivistes* discovered the place. After a glass or two of La Marina's excellent *Pacharán*, they'll probably tell you their forebear was Nelson himself.

Gambas Pil-Pil

This is one of Andalucía's tangiest dishes, incredibly simple to make and impressive to serve. It's also extremely anti-social, on account of the liberal amounts of garlic used per serving! Ideally, it should be prepared and served in individual, earthenware ramekins, which will retain the heat and allow the dish to continue sizzling after the prawns have cooked. This sizzling is the pil-pilando *sound of its name. You can vary the amounts of garlic, chilli and paprika according to your pain threshold. The ingredients given here will make a medium-hot pil-pil.*

(Serves 1)

olive oil

4 tablespoons olive oil
6–8 fat prawns, peeled
½ teaspoon paprika
1 garlic clove, chopped
1 teaspoon red chilli, finely chopped
½ teaspoon parsley, chopped

Heat the oil in the ramekin until it starts to smoke. Now add the prawns, the paprika, the garlic and the chilli and, stir-frying, move all the ingredients around together. Cook over a high heat for two to three minutes, depending on the size of the prawns, and turn the prawns over halfway through this cooking time.

Sprinkle with the chopped parsley and bring to the table, still sizzling, and serve with good chunks of bread to mop up the delicious garlicky oil.

touring around

Gibraltar

Sightseeing in La Línea is only for the dedicated; one of the town's main attractions however, for locals and visitors alike, is the **Pryca** hypermarket located at the northern end of town—it's signposted everywhere. The obvious place to 'do' is **Gibraltar**. No room here for its fascinating, tangled history (for that you'll need the Cadogan Guide to *Southern Spain*), but a word about the present-day town. Despite a certain amount of bad press, Gibraltar is still much more than just a perfect replica of an English seaside town. The town is long and narrow, strung out along Main Street with most of the shops and pubs. The harbour is never more than a couple of blocks away, and the old gates, bastions and walls are fun to explore.

Most importantly, you'll need your **passport**. Then decide whether you want to drive in—you can often drive straight in across the frontier with no queue, only to discover there's a wait of an hour or more to drive out again. Alternatively you can leave your car under the watchful eye of a parking attendant, or in a covered garage, on the Spanish side of the gates, and walk across.

Once through passport control, if you're on foot, you can either take a cab into town—5 minutes, about £3—or walk. It will take you 15 minutes at a brisk pace, but there's the thrill of walking right across the runway of Gibraltar's very unconventional airport.

the Rock of Gibraltar

The short tunnel at **Landport Gate** will probably be your entry point into town whether driving or walking; dating from the 18th century, it was for a long time the only entrance by land. It leads to **Casemates Square**, one-time parade ground and site of public executions, and now an active trading centre. **Grand Casemates** itself, part of the town's defences and barracks, provides seedy accommodation for Gibraltar's 4000-strong Moroccan labour force, but there are plans to revamp the whole area. **King's Bastion** is now used as an electricity generating station, but probably started out as an ancient Arab Gate, added to by the Spanish in 1575, and further extended in the 18th century by the British under General Boyd. It played an important defensive role at the time of the Great Siege (1779–83) by the French and Spanish, and it was from this spot that General Elliott commanded during the fierce fighting in 1782. **Ragged Staff Wharf** takes its name not from the sartorial deficiency of its troops, but either from the flagstaff that marked safe passage into the harbour, or from an emblem on the arms of the House of Burgundy, to which King Charles V belonged.

Near the centre of town, off Line Wall Road, you should spare a few minutes for the small but excellent **Gibraltar Museum**, 18–20 Bomb House Lane (*open Mon–Fri 10–6, Sat 10–2; closed Sun*), which offers a painstakingly detailed room-sized model of the Rock as it was in the mid-1800s, and a thorough schooling in its complicated history. The museum is built over the remains of a Moorish bath, with Roman and Visigothic capitals on its columns. It also contains a replica of the female skull found in Forbes Quarry in 1848, a find that predates the Neanderthal skull found in Germany by eight years. (Perhaps Neanderthal Man should be known as Gibraltar Woman.) Other exhibits include archaeological finds from Gibraltar's caves; an Egyptian mummy found floating in the Bay by local fishermen, dating from 750 BC and probably from Thebes; a natural history collection; and a gallery devoted to Gibraltar artists—among them Gustavo Bacarisas, Mania and Olimpia Reyes.

In Library Street, in the grand building that was once the Governor's Residence, is the **Garrison Library**, built during the Great Siege in the hope of preventing boredom in sieges to come. Here there are extensive archives on Gibraltar's history. Nearby are the offices of *The Chronicle*, which reported Nelson's victory at Trafalgar. The **Supreme Court** looks diagonally across the street to the former 16th-century Franciscan convent, now the **Governor's Residence**, where the changing of the guard takes place (*check with tourist office for times*). If it's bucketing down, an occurrence frequent in winter months, you can watch these serious proceedings from the warmth and comfort of the *Angry Friar*, the pub on the corner. **Southport Gate**, at the top of Main Street, was built in 1552 during the reign of Charles V and has additions from the 19th century; the wall stretching east from the gate is **Charles V's Wall**, which ends just short of the water catchments at **Philip II's Arch**. Beyond the gate you can wander through shady little **Trafalgar Cemetery**, where sad little inscriptions tell of children killed by disease, and of young men who met their bloody end at sea. The **Alameda Gardens**, a few yards away, are more cheerful; you can stop in to see the exotic flora before taking the cable car up the Rock to the Apes' Den (*leaves every 15 mins 9.30–6; £4 inc adm to nature reserve; children half-price—but leave plenty of time, for there's often a long queue*).

The cathedral of **St Mary the Crowned** (between Main Street and Cannon Lane) stands on the site of the chief mosque of Gibraltar, of which some remains can still be seen. The Anglican cathedral of the **Holy Trinity** (off Main Street, near the museum) was consecrated in 1838, and in Engineer Lane the **Great Synagogue**, rebuilt in 1768, is attended by Gibraltar's 700-strong Jewish community. **King's Chapel**, part of the Franciscan convent, was one of the few buildings left standing at the end of the Great Siege, and was an earlier sanctuary for those sheltering from the attack by Barbarossa and his pirates, although the place itself was looted. Legend has it that the chapel is haunted by the grey nun, Alitea de Lucerna, whose family forced her into convent life because they disapproved of her lover. He, however, managed to sneak into the convent, dressed as a Franciscan friar, and the two continued their relationship until, inevitably, they were discovered. The lover drowned as they tried to escape, and poor Alitea remained to stalk the cloisters, bemoaning her lost (if not unrequited) love.

The famous silhouette of the **Rock** itself, surprisingly, does not hang over the seaward edge, but faces backwards towards La Línea. From 427m up, the views from the upper part of the Rock are magnificent: the Costa del Sol curves away to the east, the mountains of Morocco sit in a purple haze across the narrow strait to the south; and way below, where the Mediterranean opens out into the wide and wild Atlantic, tiny toy-like craft plough through the waters in full sail. The Rock's entire eastern face is covered by the **water catchment system** that supplies Gibraltar's water—an engineering marvel to equal the tunnels. The upper part of the Rock has been turned into a nature reserve, which can be reached by cable car or through the entrance at Jews' Gate, on the hairpin bend where Engineer and Queen's Roads meet (*open daily except Sun, 9.30 to sunset; adm £3, children under 12 half-price, children under 5 free; cars £1.50*).

Aas well as panoramic views, admission to the reserve will get you a look at Gibraltar's best-known citizens. At the **Apes' Den** halfway up the Rock, you can see Barbary apes, a species of tailless macaque. These gregarious monkeys are much more common on the African side of the strait, and in Europe are unique to Gibraltar. There is an old saying that as long as they're here, the British will never leave. Understandably, they're well cared for, and have been since the days of their great benefactor, Winston Churchill. The Gibraltarians are fond of them, even though (as a local guide book solemnly notes) they 'fail to share the same respect for private property' as the rest of us. Now that most of their feeding grounds have been built over, they are on the dole, and it's fun to watch them when the official Keeper of the Apes comes round at feeding time. Legend has it that the apes, two packs of them numbering 60 in all, travel to and from their native Morocco by an underground tunnel in the rock.

Nearby are remains of a **Moorish wall** and, a short walk to the south, **St Michael's Cave**, a huge cavern of delicate stalactites, now sometimes used as an auditorium. In the 19th century wealthy merchants would rent it out for extravagant parties; it was also a favourite venue for illegal duels, away from the censorious eye of the authorities; and during the Second World War it was converted for use as a hospital. It's now used for concerts and fashion shows, but do bring a waterproof hat if you attend one of these—the roof leaks (*son et lumière shows at 11 and 4; free*).

At the northern end of the Rock, facing Spain, are the Upper Galleries, now called the **Great Siege Tunnels**, an extensive section of the original British tunnels, which were hacked and blown out of the rock during the Great Siege—the work of Sergeant Major Ince, who was rewarded for his labours with a plot of farming land and a racehorse. (Horseracing and hunting were extremely popular; the airport was once the site of a racecourse.) Open to visitors, the Galleries have wax dummies of 18th-century British soldiers hard at work digging and blowing up Spaniards. From here it's a short walk down to the **Moorish castle** probably founded in the 8th century by Tariq ibn-Ziyad, but its best-known feature, the **Tower of Homage**, dates from the 14th century when Abd Hassan recaptured Gibraltar from the Spanish. At present Gibraltar's **prison** is housed (and occupied) in the keep, but hopes are that this will be moved to a new military building. Unfortunately, some rather short-sighted town planning allowed a housing estate to be built within the castle's boundaries, again highlighting Gibraltar's acute need of space.

If all of the above sounds too much like hard work, why not confine yourself to Gibraltar's most popular activity—shopping. With no VAT, prices for tobacco and spirits are eye-poppingly low. Luxury items such as Swiss watches, Mont-Blanc pens and designer sunglasses are all bargains too. It's best to shop around and discover which shops you like (most have identical stock), but the following establishments have been tried and tested and have a good reputation. **Antiques**: Bensaquen Antiques, 290 Main Street; **cashmere**: Carruana, 181 Main Street (jerseys, suits and fabrics); **cuban cigars and perfume**: S. M. Seruya, 165 Main Street, and Stagnetto's, 56 Main Street; **gifts**: Marrache, 201 Main Street (jewellery, *objets d'art*, silver); **jewellery**: Sakata, 92 Main Street, and The Red House, 66 Main Street (cultured pearls, Cartier, Rolex); **menswear**: García, 190 Main Street (Dax, Burberry, etc); **porcelain**: Omni, 3 Main Street.

Algeciras

Ask at the tourist office what there is to see and you'll be told, 'Nothing. Nobody ever stays here.' Once you've seen the town you'll understand why: it's a dump. Nevertheless, Algeciras has an interesting history, and an attractive setting opposite the Rock of Gibraltar if you can see through the pollution. It played a significant role in the colonization of the eastern Mediterranean, becoming an important port in the Roman era. From AD 713 on, it was occupied by the Moors, and its name derives from the Arabic *Al Djezirah al Hadra* (Green Island). Today, apart from its importance as a port with regular connections to Ceuta, Tangier and the Canary Islands, Algeciras is a sizeable industrial and fishing centre.

The bustling, seedy port area holds little attraction for the visitor, although the small bazaars in the side streets, selling Moroccan leather goods, may whet your appetite for a trip across the strait—you can see Morocco's jagged, surreal peaks all along the coastal highway. It is also the centre of one of the busiest drug-smuggling routes in the world, and every stevedore and cab driver will be whispering little propositions in your ear if you look the type.

Inland, lying in a pleasantly wooded area, is **Los Barrios**, settled by refugees when Gibraltar was lost to the British; archaeological finds indicate that it was inhabited from earliest times. The parish church of **San Isidro** dates from the 18th century. There are two fairly decent beaches nearby—Guadarranque and Palmones.

On the N340 heading north, the road passes **San Roque**, with exceptional views over the bay of Algeciras and Gibraltar. Here are the ruins of Carteya, the first Roman settlement in the south of the peninsula. The 18th-century parish church of **Santa María Coronada** was built above the ancient hermitage of San Roque, and is worth a visit. This pretty little town is a welcome relief after the more sordid quarters of Algeciras, and an added bonus are the nearby clean beaches of Puente Mayorga, Los Portichuelos and Carteya.

Otherwise it's east along the N340 for the resorts of the **Costa del Sol**. **Sotogrande**, which you reach after just a few kilometres, is an old-established (by the Costa's standards), English-built *urbanización*. There isn't a great deal to see, and casual visitors are discouraged. But watch out for the notice-boards placed at the side of the *carretera* on polo days. It's a great spectacle to watch polo being played on the field down at the water's edge.

A *House & Garden Cortijo* on the Roof of the World

El Cortijo El Puerto del Negro

Remember the scene in *South Pacific* where Bloody Mary tells Joe Cable about *Bali Ha'i*? She throws back her head, smiles a toothless grin, points her leathery finger at the horizon, and bursts into song. And suddenly there it is, *Bali Ha'i*, a great rock rising out of the mist in the far distance.

In this instance, the *Bali Ha'i* is Gibraltar. Of course, few people who know Gibraltar would describe it as such but, then again, they probably haven't seen it from the terrace of El Puerto del Negro, 1000m above sea level on a ledge of the Sierra del Hacho.

On a clear day, Gibraltar rises from the sea, way below you and some 50km in the distance, like an enchanted island, a mythical, lost city, not quite to be believed. An occasional wisp of cloud appears from nowhere, hovers above it like a curl of sweet tobacco smoke from an expensive cigarette, then is gone.

And beyond the Rock, on the far horizon, you can see the North African coast, as far as the Atlas, a haze shimmering in a sky of the palest blue.

El Puerto del Negro owners Tony and Christine Martin found this spectacular corner of Andalucía after many years based in Singapore and the Far East. In a job which involved travelling the world for 15 years, Tony had learned the hard way exactly what constituted a good hotel, and here in the Sierra del Hacho he and Christine put their experience to the test.

After years of toil, dedication and near ruin—the floods of 1989 all but washed it away—the *cortijo* (farmhouse) finally opened for business at Christmas 1993. And, just as El Puerto del Negro had been a refuge some 500 years ago for the Moors driven out from Ronda, so today it has become a haven for discerning travellers who come from far and wide for the view, the hospitality, and Christine Martin's irresistible cooking.

This is a *cortijo* with latterday Spanish pizzaz; an Andalucian country house faithful to its surroundings but oozing contemporary style and good taste. You will know instinctively that everything here is *right*.

getting there

Cortijo El Puerto del Negro is located on the MA512 between the villages of Gaucín and El Colmenar.

From the eastern Costa del Sol, take the MA539 from San Luís de Sabinillas, 11km west of Estepona, as far as Gaucín. Turn left at the village and follow the C341 past the petrol station and out of Gaucín. After 2km, take the right fork, the MA512 towards El Colmenar. About 2km along this road, a sign on the left directs you to the Cortijo, along an unmade road. *Don't forget to shut the gate behind you!*

From Algeciras and the western Costa del Sol, take the C3331 to Jimena de la Frontera then the C341, forking left on to the MA512 3km before you reach Gaucín.

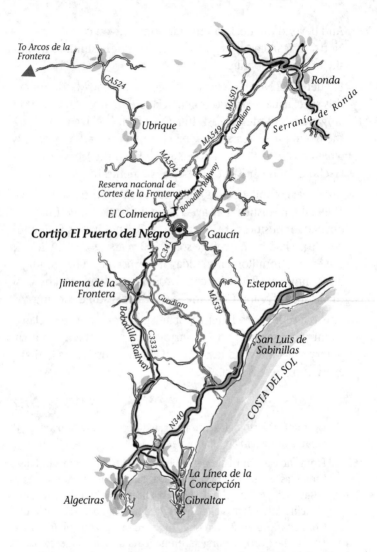

For a scenic route from Ronda, follow the C341 via Gaucín (*see* p. 163). Alternatively, you can take the train from Ronda to El Colmenar (Gaucín's official station) and then a taxi to the Cortijo (*see* touring around, below).

Cortijo El Puerto del Negro

29480 Gaucín (Málaga), ℂ(95) 215 1239. Open daily; by reservation only—booking essential. Menu 3500 pts.

The elegant, mahogany reception desk is usually unmanned but a sixth sense alerts Tony Martin to your arrival. You'll appreciate his warm welcome after a long drive here, as he takes you through the Cortijo's stylish drawing room and offers you a drink from the discreet, well-stocked bar. The Cortijo operates an honesty system, so although Tony is usually on hand to pour drinks, you're quite welcome to help yourself; just try to remember what you've had!

Then, drink in hand, walk out on to the terrace for your first glimpse of *that* view. You'll need a few moments to take it all in, before you stop to acknowledge the other guests. Because this is a small and intimate place, sometimes with no more than half a dozen guests in the restaurant, Tony and Christine do make some effort to introduce people to one another. If you are terribly shy, or simply do not wish for the company of others, a smile will suffice and you will not be bothered again. On the other hand, this is a relaxed and idyllic setting in which to meet fellow travellers, and many lasting friendships have been forged on the Martins' terrace.

After an hour or so of good conversation and two or three *gin tonicas* poured with a lavish hand, lunch is served. The dining room is bright and airy with views on three sides, good antique furniture, and a fine collection of English silver on the two sideboards. Pink and white tablecloths and starched linen napkins give lunch an air of occasion, while the sunny aspect of this lovely room keeps the mood relaxed and informal.

While her cooking is not overtly Spanish, Christine makes the most of local and seasonal produce. As she herself says, she is not out to compete with the local *comedor* which can knock up lunch for a thousand pesetas; the Puerto del Negro experience is a one-off, and unashamedly so. Moreover, the menu is fixed and there is no choice, although with a bit of notice Christine will satisfy almost any request or dietary requirement.

'Chilled avocado soup' is a favourite summer starter; the fleshy, naturally creamy avocados grown in the local *huertas* are light years away from the bland and watery varieties reserved for export.

Then comes a dish such as 'honey-glazed duck with ginger and grapefruit', pink and tender duckling with skin caramelized to perfection, then the sweetness of the bird subtly checked by the bitter tang of Seville grapefruit. And because Christine Martin is an old-fashioned cook in the very best sense, don't be surprised at the heaps of vegetables—including a mountain of crispy potatoes roasted in duck fat—which accompany the main course.

You'll have absolutely no room left for dessert, of course. That is, until the arrival of *crêpes de fresas*, strawberry crêpes, persuades you otherwise.

The Martins are rightly proud of their wine list. They specialize in selected small vineyards, usually in Navarra or Rueda, with hardly a Rioja in sight. The mark-up is low and guests get to sample excellent, lesser-known Spanish wines from 1000 pts a bottle. No wonder lunch at El Puerto del Negro often goes on until 6pm.

Crêpes de Fresas

The plump, sweet, juicy, deep-red strawberries, grown in the market gardens of Andalucía, are the inspiration behind this magnificent dessert, as prepared by Christine Martin.

(Makes about 12 pancakes)

For the crêpes:
100g/4oz plain flour
1 large egg
25g/1oz caster sugar
85ml/3fl oz milk, mixed with
25g/1oz unsalted butter, melted
85ml/3 fl oz water

For the orange brandy butter:

100g/4oz butter, softened

100g/4oz icing sugar, sieved, plus extra for dusting

3 tablespoons brandy

grated rind of 1 orange

For the filling:

450g/1lb strawberries, hulled and halved

Mix together all the ingredients for the crêpes, beating really well. Let the batter rest for at least an hour. Then make about 12 thin crêpes by pouring modest quantities of batter onto a hot, buttered griddle pan. Stack the crêpes on a plate and cover with a damp teatowel until ready to use.

Next, make the orange brandy butter. Put the butter into a bowl and beat well with a hand-held whisk, gradually adding the icing sugar. Pour in the brandy a spoonful at a time, beating all the time. Add the grated orange rind. Chill. Now put a spoonful of the softened orange brandy butter into the centre of each crêpe, together with two or three strawberries. Wrap the crêpe around the filling to form a parcel. Arrange in a shallow, buttered, ovenproof dish and chill.

Preheat the oven to 180°C/350°F/gas mark 4. Bake the crêpes in the oven for 15 minutes, then serve immediately with a fine dusting of icing sugar.

---

touring around

Although it may require some organization, one of the unsung delights of this spectacular region is a ride on the **Bobadilla railway** between Gaucín and Ronda. Rather confusingly, Gaucín's station is located in the village of **El Colmenar**, some 12km away, but it is convenient for El Puerto del Negro, which lies between the two. The hour-long train ride is sheer joy, chugging round mountain peaks, across valleys and through the tunnels of the **Serranía de Ronda**. A midday train from Ronda will get to El Puerto del Negro in time for lunch; an evening train will take you back again. Phone the Cortijo for accurate information, and to book a taxi for you from the station.

Take an hour or two to walk around the white village of **Gaucín**. It was settled in antiquity (to which Visigoth and Roman remains bear testimony), flourished under Moorish occupation, and found favour again after the reconquest. Today, a sizeable ex-patriate community has brought new prosperity to Gaucín; its narrow streets are packed with cars and the silence of the once sacred siesta hour is shattered by the unholy revving of motor-scooters.

The church of **San Sebastián**, built in 1505 with 17th-century additions, boasts three naves, and is an interesting example of Spanish Baroque style with classical elements. The **Fuente de los Seis Caños** (Fountain of Six Jets), which occupies a recess off the main square, was built of local sandstone in 1628 and has six gargoyle-like faces spouting water. The handsome **Convento de las Carmelitas**, a classical monastery built in 1704, is now the local *Casa de la Cultura.*

While walking through the village, look out for some of Gaucín's produce: several households keep bees and the local honey is justly famous in Málaga province. So are the spicy local sausages. *Rosco blanco*, a local sweetmeat akin to a doughnut, is also highly prized, but definitely not recommended for heartburn sufferers. At the end of the village, approached by a steep incline, lies the **Castillo del Aguila** (Eagle's Castle). This 10th-century Arab fortress, which commands a magnificent view over all the surrounding countryside, is in ruins, but its imposing walls and the sombre **Torre de Homenaje** still stand. Inside the fortress, a shrine was built in the 17th century, the **Ermita de Santo Niño**. The intricate plasterwork which adorns both the side chapel and the cupola is still intact.

If you're returning to the coast, there are several roads back down from El Puerto del Negro. On the way you may wish to explore the villages of **Jimena de la Frontera** or **Manilva** (*see* p. 164), or even take a longer route by way of **Ronda** (*see* pp. 172–3). If you are heading north, continue on to El Colmenar and take the MA504 in the direction of **Ubrique**. This magnificent road winds through the **Cortes de la Frontera National Park**, studded with forests of chestnut, holm-oak and *pinsapo*, the stately Spanish fir-tree.

Ubrique, a growing industrial town known for its leather goods, hangs dramatically over the Río Majaceite. From here, it's just a short ride to the lovely white town of **Arcos de la Frontera** (*see* pp. 114–15), thence onwards and upwards for the fleshpots of Jerez and Sevilla.

An 18th-century Oil Mill in the Serranía de Ronda

Awesome is a word much overused these days, but none better describes the great vistas on the road from Ronda across the Serranía to Benalauría. This is a switch-back drive so thrilling, you'll need a great deal of faith in the person at the wheel, because like the passengers, the driver is going to be scanning this landscape in amazement. Vast, imposing and strange, it is by turn both lush and lunar.

A mere hour from the Costa del Sol, 45 minutes from Ronda, a concealed turning off a mountain road takes you down through the valley of the Genal river. The road plunges down at an alarmingly steep angle through forests of chestnut, ilex and cork, eventually reaching the whitewashed *pueblo* of Benalauría below. Its alleyways and fountains betray its Arab origins, but it's a pocket-size place. The main square holds three cars—at a pinch.

mesón la Molienda, Benalauría

Park outside the village and explore on foot. La Molienda is the second house on the left as you enter Benalauría, situated above the disused oil mill from which it takes its name. In colloquial Spanish, *molienda* also means 'weariness'. If this sums up your state after an exhilarating but somewhat enervating drive here, sit down in one of the wicker chairs on the patio and order a *tinto de verano*: it will soon revive you.

getting there

From Ronda, take the C341 in the direction of Atajate and Gaucín; follow this road for 27km, turning left at the sign to Benalauría. The village lies 2km away, via a very steep descent. (N.B. Don't be confused by the earlier sign off the C341 to Benadalid—that's another place entirely.)

From Cádiz and the western Costa del Sol, follow *either* the C3331 to Jimena de la Frontera, taking the right fork just before the town on to the C341; bypass Gaucín, continuing on the C341 until reaching the sign to Benalauría on your right; *or*, from the Estepona area, take the MA539 at (San Luís de) Sabinillas, and climb through Manilva to Gaucín, continuing on the C341 to Benalauría. This road has recently been rebuilt after the floods of 1989 more or less washed it away, and it now offers the most direct—and one of the most scenic—routes from the coast to the western Serranía.

Mesón La Molienda

Calle Moraleda 59, Benalauría (Málaga), © (952) 215 2548. Open daily year round; phone to check; book at weekends. About 2500 pts.

In cooler weather the shady patio of La Molienda offers an attractive place to eat and drink. But in the summer months the heat penetrates everywhere in the open air and the two indoor dining rooms offer welcome relief. The one to the right with its railway-carriage layout is perhaps less appealing, but the smaller room, up three steps to the left, is magical. Here is a cabin in the sky which brings to mind a Moorish legacy: there are intricate Moroccan lamps and brilliantly-dyed Berber weaves, as well as a few decidedly un-Moorish wooden carvings—the sort of tat you could find in the gift section of any large department store. A thatched awning over the bar, more Tahiti than General Tarik, but nonetheless decorative, completes the eclectic interior. Best of all, however, is the square garret window, with its views across the Serranía to Alpandeire, Faraján and half a dozen other speckled white hamlets in the distance.

At the bar, the *tapas* change daily. To accompany an apéritif before getting down to the serious business of lunch, you might choose a *tapa* of tunny with potato and onion; pink, sautéed kidneys in a rich onion gravy; or a light salad of quail's eggs and pimento. If you prefer, you may order a larger *ración* as a first course to eat at the lunch table.

If you choose instead from the menu, you might start with *sopa de abuelo*, the rather unappetizing-sounding soup of the grandfather, seen on many *listas* in southern Spain but seldom prepared as competently as at La Molienda. This is a rich, cream soup of root vegetables, such as leeks and turnips, blended with potato into a vichyssoise and served with tangy pieces of good *jamón de Serrano*. Another speciality, *olla Serrana*, is a stew of chick peas, split peas and white beans, slowly simmered in a rich stock, and spiked with cumin and turmeric. Like some of the decorations, it's a dish which draws its inspiration from Morocco, the northern coast of which can be seen from the road above Benalauría, where it runs down into Gaucín.

During your meal you will frequently pause to marvel at the view and wonder again not only at the vastness of the Serranía, but its stillness. Up here there is nothing to disturb you, except for the occasional swoop of some elegant bird of prey, or the distant sound of a housewife intoning some bars of flamenco as she hangs out her washing on the roof.

Pause too to consider wine. The list is short but a bottle of *Antonio Barbadillo*, a light, red *cosecha* from Cádiz province, will prove an excellent lunchtime choice. It's one of the most expensive on the list, but still costs less than 1000 pts a bottle!

It makes a fine accompaniment to another of La Molienda's specialities: *cordero con almendras*. This stew of baby lamb with flaked almonds has been simmering gently with tomatoes and garlic and, for a summer dish, you'll find it surprisingly light. The *filetes de pollo empanado* are escalopes of chicken breast shallow fried in breadcrumbs; the secret is to add lemon juice and a drop of water as they are frying, so they become deliciously crisp, but never dry.

For dessert, try the homemade *bizcocho*, a sponge cake with almonds and cinnamon, or some *trufas*, rounds of astonishingly rich, melt-in-the-mouth chocolate ice cream. Now that the heat of the day has passed, take yourself outside to the patio to stretch out in the sunshine, with a *café solo* in one hand and a glass of murderous *aguardiente* in the other, and decide what to do with what's left of the afternoon.

Caldereta de Cordero con Almendras

It appears in myriad forms—lamb stew is one of the staples of the Andalucian kitchen. With its long, slow cooking time, stewing was a good way to prepare mutton, or lamb which was well past its infant stage. These days, it's rare to find mutton, and Spanish lambs, like policemen, are getting younger. In fact, the quality of lamb in Spain generally is excellent. This can only add to a dish which, prepared carefully, is sublime. It has reduced cooking times significantly.

(Serves 4–6)

750–900g/1 ½–2lbs boned shoulder of lamb, cut into 2–5cm/1in cubes
2 tablespoons groundnut oil
1 large onion, chopped
20 blanched almonds, chopped
4 garlic cloves, peeled and bruised
2 tablespoons sherry vinegar
450g/1lb peeled plum tomatoes, roughly chopped
8 green peppercorns
3 cloves
a few fresh mint leaves, torn
1 bay leaf
salt and pepper
grated nutmeg or a little fresh lime juice

Put the cubes of lamb into a large, heavy-based saucepan or casserole and pour in just enough water to cover them. Bring to the boil and, partially covered, lower the heat and cook gently for about 30 minutes.

Meanwhile, heat the oil in a frying pan and fry the chopped onion together with the almonds and garlic for four or five minutes, until everything in the pan has started to brown (some cooks prefer to fry garlic unpeeled to stop it burning).

Now drain the water from the lamb and, over a medium heat, add the onion, almonds and garlic from the frying pan, scraping all the juices into the casserole. Add the sherry vinegar and turn the cubes of lamb in it for a couple of minutes.

Now increase the heat a little and add the tomatoes, green peppercorns, cloves, mint leaves, bay leaf, a good pinch of salt and a few twists of the peppermill, and 120ml/4fl oz water. Cook for two or three minutes until everything is bubbling fiercely, then reduce the heat, cover the casserole and continue cooking at a very gentle simmer for a further 40 minutes, until the lamb is completely tender. Check the consistency of the stew after 20 minutes, adding more water if necessary. Also, very young or tender lamb will cook more quickly than older lamb, so test and adjust timing and liquid accordingly.

Serve this stew piping hot with a dusting of grated nutmeg, or try the exotic old Andalucian touch of a squeeze of fresh lime just before serving.

touring around

One of the area's most rewarding places of interest is right on the Molienda's doorstep, so even the laziest have no excuse. It's the **Museo Etnográfico de Benalauría**, at Calle Alta 24, ✆ (95) 215 2548, a small museum which recreates the ancient peasant life of the *campo*. It is situated next to the *molino de aceite*, the oil mill from which La Molienda takes its name.

In the museum you will find a fascinating mixture of authentic historical artefacts from rural life, including ploughshares, threshing machines and all manner of farming implements, as well as peasant dress, and even a farm-hand's lunchbox, complete with typical contents. The carefully restored oil mill next door was built in the 18th century, although parts of the building are much older. Check out the timbers, for example, which date from the 11th century—some of them are 20m long.

If you happen to be in Benalauría on 4 August, you will witness a *feria* impressive even by Andalucía's exceptionally high standards. This is an annual feast celebrating the Reconquista which takes the form of a mock battle between the Moors and Christians. It is performed in honour of Benalauría's patron saint, Santo Domingo de Guzmán.

If you are returning to Ronda along the C341, two other white villages are worth exploring. **Benadalid** once had a Moorish palace, though it's now a cemetery, and **Atajate**, perched in a crook of the Serranía, is a blindingly-white, spotless village with an air of unreality that may give you the impression that you are on a film set. A couple of local *tenderos* here sell good virgin olive oil.

For those returning to the coast, there is a choice of two routes, each quite different and offering their own delights. Nature lovers should take the first. Return from Benalauría to the 'main' road, the C341, and at the T-junction turn left. At Algatocín, turn left at the small sign for Estepona. This brings you onto the MA536/557, a long, slow, winding descent of 45km to the coast just west of Estepona. It is an unforgettable drive, passing through three distinct regions. The first is densely wooded, dropping down through forests of cork and ilex into the valley of the Serranía at **Jubrique**, an enchanted hamlet which seems somehow detached from the rest of the world. Go soon,

turn-mill at the Museo Etnográfico de Benalauría

however: there is a plan afoot to build a dam across the Genal river here, as part of a wider scheme to relieve Andalucía's chronic water shortage. Jubrique will never be the same again.

Continuing south, the landscape flattens out, with vivid green fields and gentle streams running along the plains between the sierras. Finally the road turns uphill once again, climbing through the **Sierra Bermeja**, before spitting you out on the other side, high on a ridge above the sparkling Mediterranean.

The second route allows you to explore the Roman settlement of Manilva. Turning left on to the C341, follow the road to **Gaucín** (*see* pp.155–6), and negotiate your way through the town, following signs to the MA539. After a gentle descent of some 20km through magnificent scenery, the road comes to Manilva.

The partially excavated Roman villa of **Torrejón** lies 10km north of Manilva on the MA545, back towards Gaucín, but is extremely difficult to find. An uphill gravel path heading west off the main road leads to a farmhouse: if the farmer is at home, he will direct you. It's a climb of about 1.5km from here, through fields and dense brush to the villa's hilltop site. If there is no one at home, you'll need a great deal of intuition—and luck—to find it.

Just before you enter this bustling small town of **Manilva**, turn left at the sign to the Roman Oasis restaurant (a kitsch neo-Roman 'theme' restaurant, completely un-Andalucian but with surprisingly good food, and worth visiting if you are spending time in the area), and follow the dirt track past the quarry. Where the track forks at the river, turn left for the **Roman Baths of Hedionda**, about 2km further along the road.

Other sights around Manilva include the **aqueduct**, 1km further along the river bank from the Roman Oasis.

Once you've passed through Manilva, you're within spitting distance of the coast. A gentle descent, a couple of easy bends, and you join the N340 *carretera* once again at the resort town of Sabinillas. Or you can continue past the Roman baths and aqueduct: this scenic road eventually reaches the *carretera*. After the calm of the Serranía, it will feel like another world down here.

A Hunting Lodge on the Ronda Road

el coto

There's Flamingo Road, there's the Yellow Brick Road and, if you happen to live in this corner of southern Spain, there's the Ronda Road. In these parts, the same abstracted optimism is attached to it as to any fictional highway. From its roots by the coast in the resort town of San Pedro de Alcántara, it rises like a serpent from a basket, coiling outwards and upwards to the pipe-call of the invisible snake-charmer in the mountains.

Up and up it goes, spiralling through the sierras; no hairpin bends these, but swooping, voluptuous curves making their languid, 50km ascent to the town of Ronda. The air is heavy with the scent of pine and eucalyptus and, in spring, wild flowers abound. The Ronda Road is the very staircase to heaven.

A couple of kilometres after you leave the coast in the direction of Ronda, the whole landscape changes. Wave goodbye to *costa* life at the sickly pea-green BP gas station, then up a hill, down a dale, and you're on your way. Here and there the developers have tried to make their mark, with some authentic looking *pueblos* crouched in a crook of the hills. But it makes no difference, the landscape is too vast and too proud. You've passed the last *ceramica*, the lines of low-built houses peter

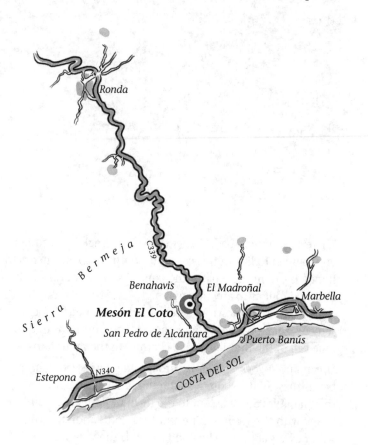

out, and now even La Heredia too is gone, a *pueblo* all the colours of a child's paintbox. Breathe in and feel the freedom of the Ronda Road.

In the sierras above the coast, where the only sounds are of birds and occasional gunshot, hunting lodges are two a penny. Some ruined, most damp, all crumbling. But there's one exception—El Coto, now transformed into a restaurant and definitely one worth breaking your journey for. Its speciality is grilled fish and succulent grilled meats.

Come for a late lunch, stay until the cool of evening, then continue to Ronda at your own pace. In all of Andalucía, there's no nicer way to spend a day.

getting there

El Coto is located on the west side of the C339 7km fom San Pedro de Alcántara (on your left if you are travelling from the coast towards Ronda). It is extremely easy to find in daylight.

From the western Costa del Sol and Estepona, head along the N340 towards San Pedro, following the Ronda sign that appears just after you have passed under the colossal white arch across the main road as you enter the town. Follow this road until it joins the C339, turning left for Ronda. El Coto will appear around a bend on your left about 5km after joining this road.

From the eastern Costa del Sol, coming from Málaga and Marbella, head west along the N340 in the direction of San Pedro. Turn right at the first sign to Ronda, just before you enter San Pedro. This bypasses the town and becomes the C339. About 7km after turning right, you will see El Coto round a bend on your left.

If your journey starts in Ronda, take the C339 to San Pedro de Alcántara. El Coto is approximately 44km along this road on your right, just after the first entrance into El Madroñal appears on your left.

Mesón El Coto

El Madroñal, Carretera de Ronda (Málaga), © (95) 278 6688. Open daily 1–4pm and 7.30–11.30pm. Set menus from 2800 pts. À la carte 4000–4500 pts.

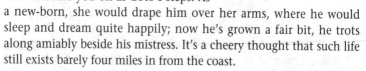

When did you last go to a restaurant to be greeted by a goat? The car park attendant at El Coto, a delightful gentleman full of wit and local wisdom, gave his 10-year-old daughter a baby goat for Christmas. So, if school's out, the chances are that she and her *cabrito* will welcome you on El Coto's steps. As a new-born, she would drape him over her arms, where he would sleep and dream quite happily; now he's grown a fair bit, he trots along amiably beside his mistress. It's a cheery thought that such life still exists barely four miles in from the coast.

El Coto's big enough to sport a car park, but it's neither posh nor fancy. It's a happy marriage between Spanish good taste and an expert Belgian management team. Walk in and you'll fall for it immediately; it's old, it's refined, the bar and dining room are handsomely proportioned, and there's a huge charcoal grill with all manner of good things sizzling upon it to whet your appetite. There's also a fine selection of ham, sausage, cheese, oils and wines—all for sale—for you to inspect while you enjoy an *aperitivo* at the bar.

The waiters are rather dashing in their long, green aprons: dashing in both senses, for there's always the agreeable buzz of high-level activity here—quite appealing when a restaurant's as well run as this one. One of the boys in green will eventually show you to your table, though while sipping an icy glass of El Coto's home-prepared *Vermut*, you may be in no hurry to leave the bar.

In the summer months, you'll sit outside on El Coto's magical, vine-covered terrace, the Sierra Bermeja above you, the deep blue Mediterranean wide and sparkling beneath you. It's an inspiring setting, one worthy of the lunch you're about to eat.

El Coto has a summer and winter menu, as well as special dishes of the day. In summer, the tone is lighter, with starters such as cold soups, *tartara de salmon* and some truly memorable salads, such as their *ensalada de langostinos y aguacates*—a simply magnificent arrangement of creamy, pale green avocado from the restaurant's own *huerta*, long, sensuously curvaceous, Baroque-looking prawns, and melt-in-the-mouth quail's eggs.

Main courses for the summer months might be *rape en salsa de cebollinos y puerros*, flavoursome monk-fish in a leek and chive sauce, or *conejo del campo al tomillo fresco*, wild rabbit with thyme. These dishes, which pay homage to both the sea and the mountains, have all the freshness and flavour of Andalucian home-cooking about them, but the panache with which they are prepared and served owes everything to a very accomplished chef and kitchen staff. To lunch on this terrace bathed in the sights, sounds and smells which typify southern Spain, is to experience the region at its very best.

In the winter, the mood changes entirely, but is no less special for that. This, after all, is a hunting lodge—and the winter menu reflects it. To start, a hearty *tabla de Ibericos,* or Spanish platter, featuring fine Serrano ham, *pata negra* (Andalucía's celebrated 'black leg' ham from the acorn-fed red Iberian pig), and a choice of gutsy *chorizos*; *morcilla de cebolla a la brasa*, a feisty, homemade onion black pudding seared on the charcoal grill (and Ronda is famous for its black pudding); or meaty snails *a la borgoña*. From late September, game birds make their appearance: partridge, pheasant, snipe and the occasional woodcock, roasted, stewed, pickled or *a la brasa*—char-grilled. The atmosphere inside the restaurant is cosy; there's an olive-wood fire blazing, while sheaves of corn hanging alongside plaits of garlic and dried chillies give the place an agreeably rustic air—it's a bit like a rather exclusive harvest festival.

El Coto has a reliable if conventional wine list and a good policy of promoting a Wine of the Month: one such offering, a ruby *Yllera, Cosecha* 1991, makes for good year-round drinking, albeit that at around 1600 pts it's no bargain in these parts.

Whatever time of year you visit, order dessert. You'll rarely see such an imaginative selection: lemon or raspberry sherbert will tickle the tongue and refresh you (the accompanying glass of vodka or *Cava* may put you back to sleep); *crema quemada*, a kind of *crème brulée* with a good burnt top for the sweet tooth; and a first-class *queso de oveja*, locally-made sheep's cheese, for the savoury.

Digestivos from a trolley which looks as if it means business may finish you off entirely; some *melón* or *licor de almendras*, a local almond liqueur, should do the job effectively.

Conejo al Tomillo

Thyme, that most aromatic of herbs, grows wild on hillsides all over Andalucía. Rabbit is the main 'bag' of the Andalucian weekend hunter and nowhere is it more hunted than in the Sierra Bermeja, the rugged, verdant hills between Ronda and the coastal plain. There's a natural affinity between the two, superbly demonstrated by this simple dish.

(Serves 4)

4 large rabbit joints
250ml/8fl oz olive oil
1 garlic clove, peeled and crushed
6 sprigs of fresh thyme
1 bay leaf
salt and pepper
rabbit liver, if available
1 teaspoon paprika
1 teaspoon cumin
2 tablespoons cider vinegar
300ml/½ pint chicken stock
1 tablespoon flour

Thoroughly wash the rabbit joints in cold water and pat dry with kitchen paper. Now prepare a marinade using the oil, garlic clove, two of the sprigs of thyme (use dried if fresh is not available—but make sure the dried is 'fresh' as it loses its flavour quite quickly), and the bay leaf. Salt and pepper the rabbit pieces on both sides and pour the marinade over them. Leave to stand for a couple of hours, or longer if possible.

When you are ready to start cooking, heat a flameproof casserole, put in the rabbit pieces (but reserve the marinade) and sauté them lightly for seven to eight minutes on each side, until they have turned golden. Remove them to a warm dish. If you've been lucky enough to get hold of a rabbit liver, chop it finely or purée it in a food processor. Off the heat, put a tablespoon of the marinade into the casserole, scrape down the juices and blend with the puréed liver, the paprika and the cumin.

Now, return the rabbit to the casserole, add the rest of the thyme, turn up the heat and, when it starts to sizzle, add the vinegar. Boil off the vinegar on a high heat for a couple of minutes, then reduce to medium and cook for a further 15 minutes, turning the rabbit once halfway through the cooking time. (If the rabbit is very wild, you may need to increase the cooking time by five minutes or so.)

Now remove the rabbit to the serving dish. Drain off the fat and, off the heat, work flour into the remaining juices using a whisk. Back over a low heat, slowly add the chicken stock and work into a rich gravy. Pour over the rabbit and serve immediately.

touring around

The area across the Ronda Road from El Coto, **El Madroñal**, is a splendid residential estate which houses some of Spain's most beautiful homes. Light years away from the samey *urbanizaciónes* along the Costa, Madroñal's houses have not been 'developed' but privately built, each one along the lines of a grand Spanish *cortijo* standing in its own extensive grounds. You may not be able to see into the houses, but the views from the streets of El Madroñal are magnificent.

From El Coto, one choice is to head for the coast, where travelling west you could make the short 8km ascent to **Benahavis**. It's a delightful whitewashed village in the Sierra Bermeja, and is a self-styled artist's colony. Although now slightly overexposed to visitors, it's a pleasant place to wonder round, with its art galleries and craft shops. To reach Benahavis, bypass San Pedro following signs for Algeciras. About 2km beyond San Pedro, just after Guadalmina, you will see the big roadsign for the right-hand turning to Benahavis.

Continue along this road for 8km to the village. Don't worry, you can't get lost—the road doesn't go anywhere else and it ends at the village. (For other coastal exploration within striking distance of El Coto, such as Marbella and Puerto Banús, *see* pp. 179–81.) On the other hand, you may want to continue climbing on the C339 to Ronda. There are no sights *per se* to see along the way, except for the beauty of the route. You'll reach Ronda in under an hour. Your first view of it as you come round a bend some 3km before the town will delight you.

With a population of some 45,000, **Ronda** is the only city in these mountains, the Ronda Serranía. It's a beautiful place, blessed with a perfect postcard shot of its lofty bridge over the steep gorge that divides the old and new towns. Because of its proximity to the Costa del Sol, it has lately become the only really tourist-ridden corner of the interior—but the coach parties seldom venture further than the Plaza de España and the bullring. The town's monuments are few; what Fernando the Catholic didn't wreck in 1485, the French finished off in 1809. Ronda saw plenty of trouble in the Civil War, and hundreds of bodies were tossed into the gorge.

The town's remarkable situation, perched atop a rocky mountain split by a 90m gorge, is the first of its attractions. You'll drive in across the Puente Nuevo, which joins the old and new towns. A good tip is to park in the new underground car park in the **Plaza del Socorro**. Start your visit here in the new town, and then walk back to the old. Itself a handsome, modern square with a recently restored church, this is the centre of the new town and residential Ronda. To orientate yourself, leave Plaza del Socorro by the northwest corner and head two blocks to the **Alameda del Tajo**, a park on the edge of the **Mercadillo**, as the new town is called. This garden has fountains, trees, plants and birds galore and, best of all in summer, shade. There's also a view of the gorge. Next to it stands Spain's oldest and most picturesque bullring, the 1785 **Plaza de Toros**, the 'cathedral of bullfighting'. This is where Pedro Romero created modern-day bullfighting, *a pie* (on foot, as opposed to horseback), and introduced the red cape to the sport. The **Museo Taurino** (*open daily 10–6pm; adm 200 pts*), located inside the bullring, tells his story. These days, the bullring holds only about three *corridas* a year, but it still has great prestige.

Working your way back to the old town, next comes the Plaza de España. On the site of the old market, the brand-new **Parador** retains the original façade but is characterless behind it. Still, the view alone makes it worthwhile and a good stopping place for a drink. Next comes the **Puente Nuevo**, built at the second attempt in 1740—the first one immediately collapsed. The bridge's two thick piers descend almost 92m to the bottom of the narrow gorge, and the view is correspondingly magnificent. Crossing the bridge into the **Ciudad** (old town), a steep path heads downwards to two 18th-century palaces: the **Palacio de Salvatierra**, with its fine display of ceramic tiles (*open Mon–Sat 11–2 and 4–7; Sun 11–1pm*), and the **Casa del Rey Moro**, built in the 18th-century over Moorish foundations. The house is not open to the public and perhaps just as well: its original inhabitant, the Moorish despot Badis, was reputed to drink wine from the hollowed-out heads of his victims. From its garden, however, there's a stairway—365 steps cut out of the rock, called the **Mina**—that takes you down to the bottom of the gorge. Here there are two bridges, the Moorish **Puente de San Miguel**, and the **Puente Viejo** rebuilt in 1616 over a former Arab bridge. The well-preserved remains of the **Baños Árabes** (Moorish baths) are now open again after extensive restoration (*open Tues–Sun 10–2pm; and afternoons in summer*).

Back at the top, there is the town's main church, **Santa María La Mayor**. This graceful building, overlooking an elegant, well-proportioned square, still retains the *mihrab* and minaret of the mosque it replaced alongside its Gothic and Renaissance details. Just to the west of here, towards the Puente Nuevo, is Ronda's most important palace, the **Palacio Mondragón**, home of Fernando Valenzuela, a minister of Carlos III. Queen Isabel stayed here on a visit to Ronda: she had come to witness at first hand the crushing of a Moorish rebellion. The palace has a Baroque façade with two *mudéjar* towers, and boasts some magnificent 15th-century Arab mosaics.

Last but not least, Ronda has some of Andalucía's best **antique shops**, situated at the eastern end of the Puente Nuevo (just inside the old town). While inevitably a lot of their stock is old tat, perseverance and a tolerance for dust will be rewarded. Look out for brass, copperware, and hand-painted ceramic plates and dishes.

The Beautiful and Tanned

Los Cano

When Prince Alfonso Hohenlohe opened his Marbella Club in the mid-1950s, he could not have foreseen the tourist boom which within 20 years would overrun this sleepy coast. Much has been written about Marbella in the years since—most of it rather negative. Yet despite its tarnished image, Marbella is today one of the most agreeable resorts in Spain. Contrary to its image, it isn't glitzy—save for the boutiques and restaurants of Puerto Banús—and while the Paseo Marítimo may boast a line of state-of-the-art apartment buildings, the old town of Marbella can hold its own with the loveliest of Andalucía's whitewashed *pueblos*. Come in December, when the town's Christmas lights illuminate a crisp night sky, or in June, when Marbella's *feria* rages for five days and nights without a break, and without a tourist in sight. It will surprise you.

But the reason so many of the Costa del Sol's two million annual visitors head this way is, of course, the beach. Andalucía's climate has proved irresistible to the northern European hordes, and what was a two-month annual 'season' 20 years ago is now a year-round business for the hundreds of beach bars and restaurants along the Costa. Known locally as *chiringuitos*, these beach places range from humble shack to elaborate restaurant complete with tablecloths and chandeliers.

About 7km east of Marbella, just off the N340 *autovía* on a pleasant though unremarkable beach, lies Los Cano. Twelve years ago, when it first opened, it was so rough that, in the heat of the summer, the waiter didn't wear a shirt. A redoubtable Englishwoman who lived nearby gave owner Frederico Cano two bits of advice: tell your waiters to put their shirts on, and heat your rolls in the oven before serving them. Today, Los Cano is one of the Costa del Sol's best *chiringuitos*. With a husband-and-wife management team so intelligent and a kitchen so professional, posher establishments are hard pressed to match it. In all of southern Spain, lunches don't come lazier or more enjoyable than here.

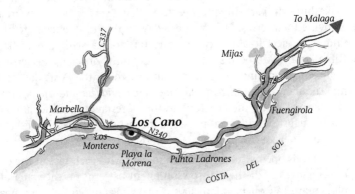

getting there

Los Cano is located on Playa la Morena (sometimes called Playa Alicate), reached via the N340 Cádiz–Málaga *autovía* (main road).

Travelling east from Marbella, watch out for the Los Monteros exit at Km187. Don't take this exit, but continue on for a further 200m, until you see a small slip road at the bottom of the hill and a sign for Los Cano. Take this slip road off to the right, and continue over two roundabouts. At the third roundabout, turn left and follow the track down to the beach. You will see Los Cano ahead of you. Travelling west from Málaga, take the Los Monteros exit at Km187. Cross the bridge over the *autovía*, then turn back onto the *autovía* in the direction of Málaga. Now continue for 200m until you see a small slip road and sign for Los Cano, and continue as above.

(*Note:* There are plans to build an *urbanización* between Los Cano and the *autovía*, so this approach road may change. The restaurant plans to keep its customers informed with up-to-date signs on the main road and beyond.)

Merendero Los Cano

Playa la Morena, Carretera Málaga–Cádiz Km187, Las Chapas, Marbella (Málaga), ✆ (95) 283 8989. Open daily 10am–11pm, but closed November. About 2500 pts.

The first thing that strikes you as you walk into Los Cano from the makeshift car park by the beach is that everybody seems to be enjoying themselves. On a winter's day on the sun-drenched terrace, under an electric-blue sky, looking out to sea with the Rock of Gibraltar and Morocco's Rif mountains on the horizon, the sense of well-being is enormous. It's hard to believe this is the Costa del Sol. In mid-summer, when Rayban Wayfarers are *de rigueur* and the beautiful and tanned lie on the beach beneath the restaurant terrace under a fierce, August sun, it's hard to escape the fact that this is well and truly the Costa del Sol—so just relax and enjoy it.

Los Cano is open virtually year round, and with each season the outlook changes as the light throws different patterns on the water and plays upon La Concha, Marbella's very own Paramount Pictures peak. The inside of the restaurant is comfortable, with high wooden beams like an Amish house, a long bar (unlike an Amish house) and the obligatory wall-mounted TV set, mercifully switched off at lunchtime.

Spaniards like to sit inside, regardless of temperature, while the glazed-in terrace is awash with almost every nationality. One of Los Cano's friendly—if overworked—waiters will show you to your table and take your drinks order. Unless you've a good reason not to, order *sangría*, Andalucía's famous fruit cup, for nowhere is it fruitier or more refreshing than here. If the red *sangría* is too heavy at lunch time, try the more unusual white, though either way *sangría*'s looks belie it: wine, brandy and fruit steeped in alcohol cannot but play the infidel.

Los Cano's fish soup is possibly the best on the coast—a feisty, fishy stock with lots of white fish added, along with generous amounts of prawns and clams. The *gazpacho*, a word these days which answers for a multitude of culinary sins, is excellent—as near a classic presentation of Andalucía's cold tomato soup as you will find, with heaps of garlic, red and green peppers, onions and breadcrumbs. (In fancier establishments these last four accompaniments are sometimes served separately from the soup.)

The wine is good and the food is cheap, so why not treat yourself to a little inter-course *entremes*, such as *boquerones al vinagre*, home cured anchovies in vinegar, or *ensalada de pimientos asados*, roast pepper salad. Some people find *sangría* too sweet to drink throughout the meal, in which case you might consider some other wine. The *Don Darias* red or white 'house' Rioja comes in at a reasonable 800 pts, while *Viña Ardanza*, a full-bodied, blackish-red wine from Rioja Alta, at 3500 pts, is one of the best bargains you'll find on any restaurant menu. As you wait for your main courses, you'll learn more about life on the Costa from other people's conversations than you would in any guide book or soap. Norwegians, Germans, Dutch, Danes, Japanese and Brits all grow more talkative as the wooden spoon sinks lower in the *sangría* jug.

Shellfish here is super-fresh; inspect the display cabinet to see what you like the look of, and order it *a la plancha* (grilled) or fried. Only the lightest sunflower oil is used for deep frying, with the result that *boquerones al limon* (fried anchovy with lemon), *calamares* (squid), *calamaritos* (baby squid), and especially Los Cano's french fries are unbeatable.

But if there's one dish which this setting really calls for it's *paella*. This dish of southern Spain has its origins in Valencia, but Almería, Málaga and Cádiz all produce marvellous variations. At Los Cano the *paellera*

comes piled high with sticky yellow saffron rice, plump, juicy morsels of chicken thigh, clams, prawns, fat mussels and slivers of red pepper—a visual as well as a culinary feast.

Eating a *paella* can take hours, and with one jug of *sangría* replacing another, it probably will. In the late afternoon the sea seems to grow calmer and more blue; the bodies on the beach are turning a nuttier shade of brown, and nobody seems inclined to do anything at all. Marbella—there's so much to see and do in the town... but give into temptation: for a mere 350 pts you too can hire a sun-lounger. Strip off, lie down, crash out—amid the Beautiful and Tanned.

Paella Los Cano

Paella *is a native of Valencia, the rice fields of which provide the base for this dish. Valencians may tell you that it is only they who can prepare* paella *and you must indulge them with a smile, for every region has its* paella. *The sticky yellow rice infused with saffron is common to them all, but each varies according to place and custom: shellfish by the sea, rabbit in the mountains and chicken wherever. Los Cano's* paella *is a combination of chicken and shellfish.*

First, you must find yourself a paella *dish, or* paellera. *These round, two-handled, iron or aluminium platters come in varying sizes to serve two people and upwards to more than 24! In Spain, you'll pick one up at any hardware store (*ferretería*) or street market. If you can't find one elsewhere, use a heavy earthenware round casserole.*

(Serves 4)

12 mussels

12 clams

4 large prawns

big pinch saffron strands

4 tablespoons vegetable oil

2 garlic cloves, chopped

1 small tin of pimientos, cut into strips

2 large tomatoes, skinned and chopped

salt and pepper

400g/14oz Spanish paella *rice or Italian arborio rice*

Paella

1 teaspoon paprika
1 litre/13/4 pints boiling water
15g/3oz frozen peas
2 lemons, each cut in half

Preheat the oven to 180°/350°F (gas mark 4). Thoroughly clean the mussels and clams with a stiff scrubbing brush, debeard the mussels and cook them with the prawns for ten minutes in a large pan of boiling water. Discard any mussels that have not opened, then prise the empty half shell from the opened mussels and discard. Meanwhile, place the strands of saffron on a sheet of foil under the grill and toast for a few seconds—no longer than 15 seconds or they will burn. Now crush the toasted strands with a pestle and mortar.

In the paellera, heat the oil and fry the garlic and pimientos for a minute or two before adding the chicken and browning it on all sides—this will take five or six minutes. Now add tomatoes and seasoning to the pan, moving the mixture around for a couple of minutes until warmed through. Next, add all the rice, spreading it evenly around the pan and sprinkling the paprika and saffron on top. When the rice has turned yellow and taken up the liquid in the pan, add half the boiling water and the peas and put the pan into the preheated oven.

After ten minutes, check the pan. The rice should have absorbed the water. Add half the remaining boiling water and cook for a further 10–15 minutes. Towards the end of this time, check the pan again, and add the remaining water if necessary. Add the shellfish—mariscos—a few minutes before you are ready to serve it, so they have a chance to reheat. Decorate the top of the dish with the strips of pimiento (if you can find them!) and the lemon halves, cover the handles of the paellera with paper napkins so you can lift it and serve immediately.

touring around

Marbella is the prettiest resort on the Costa del Sol, but it's not prettified. The growth of Puerto Banús and the various *centros commerciales* (shopping malls) up and down the coast has actually helped the old town retain its character, as the chi-chi shops of the 1970s and 1980s have moved away to more commercial areas, leaving Marbella to itself. Roman, Arab, medieval and later styles come together in a town which, given its many diverse influences, is surprisingly homogeneous.

Explore the old town. The main square, **Plaza de los Naranjos** (Orange Square), named for its rows of orange trees, is a good starting point. It contains the **Ayuntamiento** (town hall), built in 1568, Marbella's most important civil building. Inside is the **Sala Capitular** (chapter house), with a good *mudéjar* ceiling. The town hall is also home to Marbella's **Municipal Museum** (© Turismo (95) 277 1512), with its collection of Roman, Visigoth and Arab exhibits. Across the square, the **Casa del Corregidor** (magistrate's house), built in 1552, has a fine *mudéjar*-Gothic façade and Renaissance gallery.

Follow the Calles Carmen and Chinchilla east off Plaza de los Naranjos to bring you to Plaza de la Iglesia and the **Iglesia Mayor de la Encarnación**, Marbella's 18th-century parish church. It boasts a red stone portal, carved in 1756 by a celebrated local stonemason, José Gómez. It also houses a 'Sol Mayor' organ, and is the setting for occasional concerts. Continue on past the church, following signs to the **Museo del Grabado** (© (95) 277 4638). This is Marbella's print museum, housed in the 16th-century **Palacio Bazán**, with its beautiful porticoed patio and very fine *mudéjar* ceilings. You'll see works here by Picasso, Dali and Miró.

At the top of the town, Marbella's **Alcázar** marks the old town boundary to the east—a mini suspension bridge now connects it to the newer part of town—and sits handsomely surveying the scene. Back across the Avenida Ricardo Soriano, on the sea side of the main road which trundles noisily through town, the **Alameda** is a beautiful old garden with fountains, tiled benches, kiosks to buy a drink or lottery ticket, and mature old palms trees which must have seen everything in their time. It's the perfect spot for an early evening *paseo*. So is the **Paseo Marítimo**, Marbella's boardwalk, easily reached from the Alameda by continuing down the Avenida del Mar towards the sea.

For Marbella's so-called high life, check out **Puerto Banús**, the magnificent yacht harbour 6km to the west of town. No ancient fishing port this: still on the drawing board of architect Alberto Díaz Fraga in 1970, its first shops and restaurants opened for business only a year later. It has been growing ever since and—although today it's somewhat over-the-top with its glitzy restaurants, tacky piano bars and ostentatious boutiques—only a heart of stone could fail to be moved by the sheer concept of the place, its colour and light and verve, and the sight of some of the world's most magnificent yachts, sleek and silent at their moorings.

For a glimpse of how the rich really live, walk around **Puente Romano**, a village in the neo-Andalucian style. Located 500m west of the Marbella Club Hotel on the sea-side of the main *carretera* between Marbella and Puerto Banús, this made-to-look-old new village was designed in 1973 by award-winning architect Eugenio Vargas Izquierdo, and is built around the Roman bridge from which it takes its name. The bridge today links the two parts of this *urbanización*. Puente Romano is an example of just how good and imaginative latter-day Spanish design can be.

Across the road, on the mountain-side of the *carretera*, Juan Mora's modern **mosque** bears witness to the return of the Arabs to this region—after an absence of 600 years; while a few hundred metres to the west, on the road to Istan, is the Saudi royal family's residence, a fully-fledged $40-million replica of **The White House**, complete with helipads, bomb shelter and a dining room which can seat 500 guests. King Fahd himself hasn't been here in ten years—but it's always nice to have somewhere just in case.

The Arabs are not the only people to have returned after a long absence. On the eastern side of Marbella, between Los Cano and the town, on the northern side of the *carretera*, a small sign directs

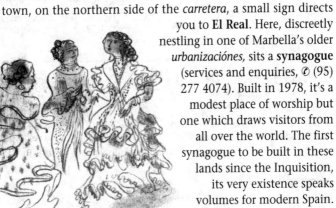

you to **El Real**. Here, discreetly nestling in one of Marbella's older *urbanaciónes*, sits a **synagogue** (services and enquiries, ℂ (95) 277 4074). Built in 1978, it's a modest place of worship but one which draws visitors from all over the world. The first synagogue to be built in these lands since the Inquisition, its very existence speaks volumes for modern Spain.

women in feria costume

A Culinary Glossary

The full Spanish culinary vocabulary is enormous, and several pocket guides are available that give extensive lists of the many terms and phrases. The following should, though, provide some of the necessary basics.

In the Restaurant

breakfast	*desayuno*	bill/check	*cuenta*
lunch	*almuerzo/comida*	change	*cambio*
dinner	*cena*	set meal	*menú del día*
knife	*cuchillo*	waiter/waitress	*camarero/a*
fork	*tenedor*	Do you have a table?	*¿Tiene una mesa?*
spoon	*cuchara*	...for one/two?	*¿...para uno/dos?*
cup	*taza*	Can I see the menu, please?	*Déme el menú, por favor.*
plate	*plato*	Do you have a wine list?	*¿Hay una lista de vinos?*
glass	*vaso*		
glass/small glass (of wine)	*copa/copita*	Can I have the bill (check), please?	*La cuenta, por favor.*
napkin	*servilleta*		
table	*mesa*	Can I pay by credit card?	*¿Puedo pagar con tarjeta de crédito?*
menu	*carta/menú*		

Entremeses y Huevos (Hors-d'œuvre & Eggs)

aceitunas	olives	*fideos*	noodles
alcachofas con mahonesa	artichokes with mayonnaise	*huevos de flamenco*	baked eggs in tomato sauce
ancas de rana	frog's legs	*gambas pil-pil*	shrimp in hot garlic sauce
caldo	broth		
camarones	fritters	*gazpacho*	cold soup
entremeses variados	assorted hors-d'œuvre	*huevos al plato*	fried eggs
		huevos revueltos	scrambled eggs

salmorejo	cold, thick tomato soup with ham	sopa de espárragos	asparagus soup
		sopa de fideos	noodle soup
sopa de ajo	garlic soup	sopa de garbanzos	chickpea soup
sopa de arroz	rice soup	sopa de lentejas	lentil

Pescados (Fish)

acedías	small plaice	langosta	lobster
adobo	fish marinated in white wine	langostinos	giant prawns
		lenguado	sole
almejas	clams	lubina	sea bass
anchoas	anchovies	mariscos	shellfish
anguilas	eels	mejillones	mussels
angulas	baby eels	merluza	hake
ástaco	crayfish	mero	grouper
atún	tuna fish	mojama	tuna (cured)
bacalao	codfish (usually dried)	navajas	razor-shell clams
		ostras	oysters
besugo	sea bream	parga	'porgy' (type of sea bream)
bogavante	lobster		
bonito	tunny	pejesapo	monkfish
boquerones	anchovies	percebes	barnacles
caballa	mackerel	pescadilla	whiting
calamares	squid	pez espada	swordfish
calamaritos	small squid	platija	plaice
cangrejo	crab	pulpo	octopus
centollo	spider crab	rape	angler-/monkfish
chanquetes	whitebait	raya	skate
chipirones	cuttlefish	rodaballo	turbot
...en su tinta	...in its own ink	salmón	salmon
chirlas	baby clams	salmonete	red mullet
cigalas	Dublin Bay prawns	sardinas	sardines
		trucha	trout
dorado	sea bass	urta	perch (type of)
escabeche	pickled or marinated fish	veneras	scallops
gambas	prawns		

Carnes y Aves (Meat and Fowl)

albóndigas	meatballs	lomo	pork loin
asado	roast	morcilla	blood sausage
bistec	beefsteak	paloma	pigeon
buey	ox	pata de cerdo	pigs trotter
cabrito	kid	pato	duck
callos	tripe	pavo	turkey
cerdo	pork	perdiz	partridge
chorizo	spiced sausage	pinchitos	spicy
chuletas	chops		mini-kebabs
cochinillo	sucking-pig	pollo	chicken
conejo	rabbit	rabo/cola de toro	bull's tail cooked
corazón	heart		with onions
cordero	lamb		and tomatoes
cordoníz	quail	riñones	kidneys
faisán	pheasant	salchicha	sausage
fiambres	cold meats	salchichón	salami
filete	fillet	sesos	brains
hígado	liver	solomillo	sirloin steak
jabalí	wild boar	ternera	veal
jamón de York	baked ham		
jamón Serrano	raw cured ham		
lengua	tongue		

Note: *potajes, cocidos, guisados, estofados, fabadas* and *cazuelas* are various kinds of stew.

Verduras y Legumbres (Vegetables)

alcachofas	artichokes	espárragos	asparagus
apio	celery	espinacas	spinach
arroz	rice	garbanzos	chickpeas
arroz mariner	rice with saffron	guisantes	peas
	and seafood	habas	broad beans
batata	sweet potato	iseber	iceberg lettuce
berenjena	aubergine	judías (verdes)	French beans
	(eggplant)	lechuga	lettuce
cebolla	onion	lentejas	lentils
champiñones	mushrooms	palmitos	hearts of palm
col	cabbage	patatas	potatoes
coliflor	cauliflower	fritas	fried
endibias	endives	salteadas	sautéed
ensalada	salad	al horno	baked
escarole	escarol lettuce	pepino	cucumber

pimiento	pepper	setas	Spanish
puerros	leeks		mushrooms
remolachas	beetroots (beets)	zanahorias	carrots
repollo	cabbage		

Cooking Methods

al horno	roasted or baked in the oven	churrasco	cooked over hot coals, Córdoba-style
a la brasa	char-grilled	cocido	boiled
a la parrilla	grilled on an iron hot-plate	empanado	fried in breadcrumbs
a la plancha	grilled		
asado	spit roast	frito	fried

Frutas (Fruits)

albaricoque	apricot	manzana	apple
almendras	almonds	melocotón	peach
cerezas	cherries	melón	melon
ciruelas	plums	naranja	orange
ciruela pasa	prune	pasas	raisins
datiles	dates	pera	pear
frambuesas	raspberries	piña	pineapple
fresas	strawberries	plátano	banana
(con nata)	(with cream)	pomelo	grapefruit
higos	figs	sandía	watermelon
limón	lemon	uvas	grapes

Postres (Desserts)

arroz con leche	rice pudding	natillas	custard
bizcocho/pastel/torta	cake	pajama	flan with ice cream
blanco y negro	ice cream and coffee float	pasteles	pastries
crema Catalana	custard with cinnamon	queso	cheese
		requesón	cottage cheese
flan	crème caramel	tarta de frutas	fruit pie
galletas	biscuits (cookies)	tocino de cielo	caramel custard
granizado	slush, iced squash	torta	shortcake
helados	ice creams	turrón	nougat

Bebidas (Drinks)

water with ice	*agua con hielo*	white	*blanco*
mineral water	*agua mineral*	vintage	*cosecha*
(without/with fizz)	*(sin/con gas)*	aged wine	*crianza*
milkshake	*batido de leche*	wine cup	*tinto de verano*
coffee (with milk)	*café (con leche)*	sherry	*vino de Jerez*
chocolate	*chocolate*	dry	*fino*
milk	*leche*	nutty	*amontillado*
tea (with lemon)	*té (con limón)*	sweet	*oloroso*
orange juice	*zumo de naranja*	Spanish	
beer (draught)	*cerveza (caña)*	champagne	*cava*
wine	*vino*	wine brandy	*aguardiente*
red	*tinto*	rum (or gin)	
rosé	*rosado*	and Coke	*Cuba Libre*

Other Vocabulary

aceite (de oliva)	(olive) oil	*migas*	fried breadcrumbs
azúcar	sugar		
adobo	marinade	*pan*	bread
ajo	garlic	*panecillo*	roll
albahaca	basil	*perejil*	parsley
bocadillo	sandwich (made from French-type bread)	*pimienta*	ground pepper
		romero	rosemary
		salsa	sauce
clavo	clove	*sandwich*	sandwich (made from English-type bread)
comino	cumin		
empanada	savoury pie		
hielo	ice	*salvia*	sage
jengibre	ginger	*(sin) sal*	(without) salt
mantequilla	butter	*tomillo*	thyme
mermelada	marmalade	*tostada*	toast
miel	honey	*vinagre*	vinegar